VOTE LIKE JESUS

Answering 15 Big Questions About God vs. Government

MARK DRISCOLL

Vote Like Jesus: Answering 15 Big Questions About God vs. Government
© 2024 by Mark Driscoll

ISBN: 979-8-9897173-7-8 (Paperback), 979-8-9897173-8-5 (E-book)

CONTENTS

CHAPTER 1: Why is the Government Against God?........1

CHAPTER 2: What Does the Bible Say About Government?. 11

CHAPTER 3: Why is America a Nation in Decline?....... 23

CHAPTER 4: What are the 2 Kingdoms?...............35

CHAPTER 5: What is the Role of Christianity in American Politics?..........................47

CHAPTER 6: What Happens to Churches That Won't Fight for the Bible?........................ 59

CHAPTER 7: Should a Christian Be a Nationalist or a Globalist?............................69

CHAPTER 8: How is Globalism a Prophetic Sign of the End Times?......................... 79

CHAPTER 9: What is the Demonic Political Spirit of Babylon?............................ 91

CHAPTER 10: What is Civil Disobedience?............ 101

CHAPTER 11: Should Christians Live Off the Grid and Ignore Politics Like the Ancient Essenes?........... 111

CHAPTER 12: Should Christians Seek to Overthrow the Government Like the Ancient Zealots?............121

CHAPTER 13: Should Christians Be a Separated Subculture Like the Ancient Pharisees?...............137

CHAPTER 14: Should Christians Become Progressive Like the Ancient Sadducees?. 147

CHAPTER 15: How Would Jesus Vote?. 163

CONCLUSION: Plug Your Nose and Vote. 173

ENDNOTES. 177
ABOUT REALFAITH. 183
MORE RESOURCES. 185

CHAPTER 1
Why is the Government Against God?

Proverbs 14:34 – Righteousness exalts a nation, but sin is a reproach to any people.

Some years ago, I was in Ohio at a coffee shop when an Amish family pulled up in a horse-drawn buggy to get drinks and snacks (and just in case you were wondering, they paid with cash and not with a credit card). They were wearing handmade clothes – the boys wearing pants with suspenders and the girls wearing dresses that covered them from head to toe. The boys wore hats while the girls wore bonnets. There was no gender confusion in this family. The family members spoke to no one, did not make eye contact, and were visibly uncomfortable. People started taking photos near their buggy and posting them on social media from their phones, and I'm unsure if the family even understood what was happening. In that moment, it felt like the past and present intersected in a most peculiar way, and as they slowly drove away, sipping on their drinks along the shoulder of the road while cars whizzed past their buggy, I thought to myself, "Most Christians are Amish and don't even know it."

The world has changed, and most Christians are

still living in the past. As a result, most Christian organizations, ministries, churches, and church leaders are ignorant, naïve, gullible, vulnerable, and living in the past while surrendering the future.

The world surrounding the Church has, in the Western world, quickly moved from positive to neutral and now negative. The magazine *First Things* describes itself as "America's Most Influential Journal of Religion & Public Life." In an article titled *The Three Worlds of Evangelicalism*, a convincing case is made that, in my lifetime, the greater cultural context in which Christianity exists, with minor exceptions in small pockets of conservative populations, has forever changed from positive to negative.[1]

Welcome to the People's Republic of America

1. *Positive World (pre-1994)* – In this period, to be a good citizen, you needed to be involved in some sort of formal religious community, like a church, because they gave us basic Judeo-Christian morals and guidelines that helped hold culture together. The 10 Commandments acted as guardrails that forbid such things as lying, stealing, adultery, and murder. Politicians, for example, were encouraged to state their belief in God and point to the church they were a part of. As a general rule, it was considered preferable to be married in a church building by clergy, have your children baptized (even as infants), and have your funeral in a church. The result was widespread cultural Christianity among people who professed a faith they neither practiced nor possessed. President George Washington said in his farewell address, "Of all the dispositions and habits which lead to political prosperity, Religion and Morality are indispensable supports...Reason and experience

2

both forbid us to expect that National morality can prevail in exclusion of religious principle."[2] The result was a diluting of the Christian faith. A clear understanding of the gospel – repentance from sin and faith in Jesus Christ – became more of a general belief in a higher power called God and decent moral behavior, which was part of one's citizenship (cultural Christianity). A century and a half later, president-elect Dwight Eisenhower said, "Our form of government has no sense unless it is founded in a deeply felt religious faith, and I don't care what it is."[3] Most Christian education (K-12, college, seminary) started during this period, along with most denominations, many church networks, Christian publishing houses, Christian churches, and Christian record labels, as this was the foundation for modern-day Evangelical Christianity. During the positive age, Christians debated secondary issues such as whether children should be baptized as babies, Calvinism vs. Arminianism, and speaking in tongues. The reason most churches, if not all, are struggling and hemorrhaging today is because they are doing life and ministry like they're on the cutting edge of the 1950s. Doing ministry in a positive world is like the days in the Old Testament when the nation of Israel, generally speaking, was under God's authority, acting in obedience to His Word.

2. *Neutral World (1994-2014)* – In this period, the cultural mood toward Christ, Christianity, and the Church became rather indifferent. No one really cared if you were married in a church or a casino; there was not widespread pressure apart from the traditional grandparents to have younger generations baptized; and you could run for political office without most people caring if you were part of a church or not. If you think of

it like a game of musical chairs, Christians had had a chair up to this point. Around this time, the metaphorical music stopped playing, they no longer had a seat, and Christianity went from the center to the periphery of cultural influence. As Christians began sensing this loss, two primary movements arose within Evangelicalism. One, the Religious Right sought to save not just Americans but also America itself by pushing back on offensive aspects of culture in every arena, from politics to education and entertainment. The thought of Christians calling themselves the "moral majority" seems a bit comical, as the majority of Americans are certainly not godly or even moral. Two, as church attendance began to decline, there was a movement of Seeker-sensitive Christianity that sought to update the Church, make it more relevant and less traditional, and operate more like a marketing business that treated people as customers to be served by large mega-churches that functioned as malls where there were stores and departments for every member of the family. They hoped they could bring people from the world back into the Church and a saving relationship with Jesus Christ by making Christianity cool, relevant, and meeting the felt needs of consumers. The downside was a weakened theological and biblical understanding by these Christians, who grew more accustomed to being entertained than taught and had a shallow understanding of Christian truths due to a weak diet with little protein from the pulpit. This led to apostasy and deconstructionism, which would soon seek to tear down every vestige of Christian truth and every remnant of Christian legacy when the negative world arrived. Christian pulpits were focused on positive and uplifting inspirational messages in the neutral world, trying to squeeze Christianity-lite into the mainstream areas of self-help, motivational life coaching, and practical principles to live by rather than a Person to live for. Life and ministry in the neutral world are a bit like the days of the New Testament, when the Roman government did not really care what Christians believed so long as they held out ultimate allegiance to the nation.

3. *Negative World (2014-present)* – In the negative world, people are no longer positive or indifferent to Christianity but instead opposed. This is because Bible-based Christianity (unlike the

apostate mainline Protestant denominations and progressive, social justice warrior, pseudo-Christian apostates) is considered immoral. The Bible is now regarded by many as an evil book filled with oppression – sexism, racism, and homophobia. Today, to be moral is not to obey the Bible but rather to oppose it, and social justice exists in large part to deconstruct or dismantle Christian beliefs and institutions by canceling leaders (which is the Left's version of crucifixion). This explains why every "former" evangelical can get their 15 minutes of fame in the godless media by trashing anything connected to Christ and gets a bonus round of coverage if they use words like "spiritual abuse," which often just means their parents spanked them. Everything from media to social media, entertainment, government schools, and Marxist universities is aligned in the fight against Biblical standards on everything from gender to sexuality, marriage, and morality. For example, most young adults in the UK today support a ban on the Bible as hate speech.[4] Today, you can get kicked off a social media platform for "hate speech" by simply reading a Bible verse without commentary. That verse does not even need to be that controversial at face value. This isn't hypothetical. I can confirm that reading 1 Timothy 5:8 will do the trick: "If anyone does not provide for his relatives, and especially for members of his household, he has denied the faith and is worse than an unbeliever." Apparently, in the negative world, telling guys to go to work so their family can live indoors and eat food that the government did not provide is offensive and intolerant. In the negative world, core bedrock, foundational, closed-handed, primary issues are under attack, including the lies that the God of the Bible is a moral monster, gay marriage is

God's will, transgenderism should be celebrated
by Christians, abortion is okay, and sin should be
tolerated instead of repented. Life and ministry in
a negative world are a lot like Joseph in Egypt,
Daniel in Babylon, and Elijah in the days when the
demons Baal and Asherah ruled politically through
King Ahab and Queen Jezebel. The problem
with a seeker approach in a negative world that
compromises on gender is that it drives away
healthy, godly men, which explains their absence
in Christian churches. If a church seeks to create
an environment where, for example, a transgender
"male" feels welcome and comfortable, every
healthy, heterosexual male will feel unwelcome and
uncomfortable, starting with the alpha male fathers
who do not want their sons to experience the
same confusion in the Church that they encounter
everywhere else. In the negative world, church
should first be for God, then for believers, and
unbelievers are welcome to come and learn how
to repent to God and walk with fellow believers.
In a negative world, the offense of the cross
cannot be lost. In a culture that offends God, the
Church must accept that it will either offend God
or culture. The Church must accept the fact that
all the verses about not being of the world and
the world hating us were meant for the negative
world, as Bible-believing Christians are now an
outcast, minority subculture. Unlike the previous
generations of Western Christians, the negative
world has declared war on the Bible and Church,
which means that playing nice, staying out of
trouble, not pulling punches, and being nuanced
and clever from the pulpit are all acts of treason
and surrender, effective immediately.

The Fall of the Culture Allows the Rise of the Church

Personally, I grew up in the negative world before the negative world permeated the entirety of America and do not understand the neutral or positive world. I grew up in a suburb of Seattle, and today, this is the least churched city in the United States of America. I got saved on a state university campus, the place where cultural decline down and to the left is always a generation ahead of mainstream culture. Brainwashed minions eventually graduate to turn the greater culture into the same sort of liberal hellscape as the government-funded campus that bred them for

bedlam. I spent roughly two decades preaching the gospel and teaching the Bible to people who were progressive, gay, and godless, giving a prophetic glimpse into the future day that is today.

Most Christian churches, ministries, and schools are built for peace time, and this worked until we entered the war time of the negative world. I've spent my entire adult life preparing for this season of the negative world. While many Christian leaders are shocked, this apostasy, decline, perversion, and openly demonic influence on every aspect of Western culture sadly seems, to those who have been in progressive strongholds, very normal. This is all I've ever known. I feel like I have come from the future, and God has been preparing me my entire life to be helpful right now. Believers can start to feel like Daniel in Babylon due to lightning rod events like the death of George Floyd, the demonic landslide of support for Black Lives Matter (which is overtly anti-fathers, anti-faith, and anti-family), Pride Month, and the DEI (Diversity, Equity, and Inclusion) mandates driving insanity in the workforce and government colleges. Additionally, the COVID season, where the demonic spirit of fear ruled the planet and closed churches at Easter for the first time in world history, caused many, if not most, pastors to become cowards, surrendering their flock to Fauci as the new global pope. Locking the church doors when people needed to worship most, demanding they get a vaccination, and mandating everyone wear a mask to worship felt a lot like the early Church, when the controlling, religious bureaucrats forcing masks became the new circumcision debate between the clean and unclean. The rest of this book will talk about the amazing opportunity God's people have to live counterculturally blessed lives under the Lordship of Christ while the surrounding culture implodes. The place of the Western Church is the same as the early Church under the declining Roman Empire, which gives us great hope that the best is yet to come for God's people regardless of what happens in the government. As people lose hope in government, they find hope in God. For this reason, the Bible tells us how God rules over government, which we will study next.

CHAPTER 2
What Does the Bible Say About Government?

Romans 13:1 – Let every person be subject to the governing authorities. For there is no authority except from God, and those that exist have been instituted by God.

There is one chapter in the Bible that is widely considered to be the most significant section about God versus government. Do you know what chapter that is? Romans 13. Unfortunately, too often, Christians only quote part of the chapter and believe the Bible commands us to obey the government without exception, which is untrue.[a]

Romans 13, along with the rest of the Bible, strikes a healthy tension between anarchy and tyranny. Anarchy is the political and social disorder that happens when there is no governmental rule of law. Tyranny is the oppressive and unjust rule of law imposed by a brutish government. To help us understand these two God-given guardrails intended to keep governments and citizens out of the ditch, we will examine this section of Scripture in detail.

[a] This chapter is an adaptation from a 365-day devotional commentary I wrote on the entire book of Romans, which you can find at realfaith.com

Romans 13:1

Romans 13:1 – Let every person be subject to the governing authorities. For there is no authority except from God, and those that exist have been instituted by God.

God's timeless Word is always timely. Because it is eternal, it always fits perfectly into any season. The question at hand in Romans 13 is an important one: How should Christians respond when there is conflict between God and government? As believers in America, we are citizens of God's Kingdom first and residents of our nation second. So, what do we do when the laws of our nation differ from God's laws?

Romans 13:1 makes it clear that every person is subject to governing authorities. But what does that mean practically? The following is a list of important truths about God's authority:

1. *God has and is ultimately the source of all authority; all other authority is derivative.* There is no one alongside or equal to God. His Word – the Bible – is our highest authority, and through it, God communicates with and convicts us.
2. *God's authority is both external and internal.* External authority comes through parents, pastors, politicians, or police officers, to name a few. Internal authority comes through the Person, presence, and power of the Holy Spirit. The flesh is our predisposition toward sin, folly, and rebellion, but if you have God's internal authority and are led by the Spirit, you don't need as much external authority.
3. *God's authority is on a continuum from parental to civil.* The first authority God establishes in

our lives is parental – we are supposed to honor our mothers and fathers. The Bible says children are born sinners and need to be born again by their Savior. They also need parental authority to help save them from foolish decisions. As a parent, if you don't instruct your children about obedience to authority, you are raising them to be bad citizens of both the state and God's Kingdom. The result is an independent generation of fools and rebels.

4. *Sin is rebellion against authority, and it is the default of our flesh.*[a] We are sinners by nature and by choice, and when we are conformed to the pattern of this world, our first instinct is to push back and bristle against or even disregard authority. We need to be transformed by the renewing of our minds and learn to relate rightly to authority in honor of God, who is over all authority.

5. *Sinners cannot and will not make a perfect system, and even if one existed, sinners would ruin it.* Every system has some measure of imperfection because imperfect people created it. Imperfect people do things imperfectly. Earth was perfect when God made it; He called it "good" and "very good." Then God handed the leadership and authority over to Adam and Eve, and they chose sin and folly. They broke the system. Humans are not the solution; they are always the problem. We need God to right everything we've made wrong, fix everything we've broken, and heal everything we've hurt.

6. *The state is God's servant.* God is the ultimate authority, and the government is under Him. We should have a general submission and respect for government as good citizens who try to

[a] 1 John 3:4

honor authority and do what is right in the sight of the law. This does not mean, however, that everything the government tells us to do should be done. There are times when our government is against God, and our higher allegiance and loyalty must be to our God above the government. There is a difference between generally respecting authority and disagreeing with a particular policy. One example is the nation of China, with a godless, communist regime, which makes it exceedingly difficult for Christians to practice their faith openly. So much of the Church is underground. From 1980 to 2015, China implemented a population control initiative known as the "One-Child Policy." Couples were only allowed to have one child, so if they became pregnant with a second child, they were expected to kill it. Could Christians obey this policy? Of course not. You can be respectful of your governing authorities but completely disagree with and disobey certain laws.

7. *New is not always improved.* Removing old authority and replacing it with new authority does not necessarily mean you get better authority. Jesus explains this problem with the principle of seven demons in Matthew 12:43-45:

> When the unclean spirit has gone out of a person, it passes through waterless places seeking rest, but finds none. Then it says, "I will return to my house from which I came." And when it comes, it finds the house empty, swept, and put in order. Then it goes and brings with it seven other spirits more evil than itself, and they enter and dwell there, and the last state of that person is worse than the first. So also will it be with this evil

generation.

Unless God is involved, change does not necessarily make things better. One historical example is Saddam Hussein. He was the horrible, godless, and demonic dictator of Iraq who thought he was the reincarnation of King Nebuchadnezzar of Babylon. While Hussein was in power, he managed to keep some semblance of peace through his dictatorial rule. He was then overthrown in 2003, and a massive power vacuum ensued. Seeking to fill that vacuum, various terrorist organizations and jihadist groups arrived on the scene. A group called ISIS rose to power and tried to create a jihadist state that ruled through imposition, threatening people with the sword. In the days of Hussein, 1.5 million Christians lived in Iraq, many of whom traced their ancestry back to the days of Jesus. When ISIS ruled, that number decreased to 150,000. Ninety percent of Christians either fled to save their lives or were put to death for refusing to deny Jesus. Am I saying Hussein was a good, godly leader? Absolutely not. My point is simply that the removal of an evil government does not guarantee a good one will fill its empty position.

8. *When Christians are responsible citizens, they enjoy greater freedom and influence.* We worship more freely and privately because we are not in conflict with the government. We also have an opportunity to earn positions of leadership in the government and society that can make a positive change on behalf of God's standards.

The Old Testament tells the story of Joseph, a Jewish young man who was betrayed by his brothers and sold into slavery.ᵃ An Egyptian governmental leader named Potiphar bought Joseph, and eventually Joseph worked his way up to be second in command to Pharaoh, who was worshiped as a god. The Egyptians recognized that Joseph was filled with the Holy Spirit and that the anointing of God was on his life, so they elevated him to a position that allowed him to care for God's people and eventually save the nation of Israel.

A second Old Testament example is Daniel, who was a young Jewish man taken to Babylon as part of the Exile. Selected for his intelligence, Daniel was sent to the equivalent of a Babylonian university to learn their ways and their language. Scripture says he lived with character and integrity and was filled with the Spirit of God. Eventually, the Babylonian king had some troubling dreams, and, out of all the "wise men" in the land, only Daniel could correctly interpret their meaning. Dreams come from God, and it took a person with the Spirit of God to interpret revelations from God. As a result, Daniel became a prominent political leader in Babylon and other nations for decades, serving under various kings and kingdoms because he conducted himself with character and integrity.

A third Old Testament example of a politically responsible believer is Nehemiah, who worked for the Persian government and served as cupbearer to the king. This was a highly trusted cabinet position because people often tried to poison the king through what he drank. While serving in this government position, Nehemiah learned that the Jews, who had returned from

ᵃ Genesis 37-50

exile to Jerusalem, were in deep trouble. His heart was broken, and he had an overwhelming desire to rebuild Jerusalem (God's city) and the Temple. Nehemiah asked the king for permission to return to his home country with the government's blessing and support, and the king granted his request to rebuild the city torn down by the Babylonian government in the days of Daniel. The Persians gave Nehemiah the necessary legal paperwork to protect him on the journey, as well as the resources and commodities needed to rebuild the city of Jerusalem and its walls. As a result, the city became fortified and protected, and the worship of God began once again in Israel.

Being a good citizen of the state does not mean we always agree with the state. It does mean, however, that we submit to the Lord as we seek to earn the freedom to worship Him and seek positions of influence to change anything that is contrary to His Word.

Why do we need a government? Because evil won't stop itself. Satan and demons are real, and so are evildoers and sinners. If you don't believe that some people are totally depraved and wicked, you are naive, gullible, and susceptible to destruction. Not everyone is good, and not everyone is safe. Evil will never stop itself, because the goal of evil is total destruction, so our God of authority works through governmental authority to restrain it.

Romans 13:2-4

Romans 13:2–4 – Therefore whoever resists the authorities resists what God has appointed, and those who resist will incur judgment. For rulers are not a terror to good conduct, but to bad. Would you have no fear of the one who is in authority? Then do what is good, and you will receive his approval, for he is God's servant for your good. But if you do wrong, be afraid, for he does not bear the sword in vain. For he is the servant of God, an avenger who carries out God's wrath on the wrongdoer.

Civil authority exists to restrain vice. The "we are good and getting better" lie is a pernicious and powerful delusion. The more we increase technology, the greater our capacity to cause human suffering and death. Counterfeit, demonic forces empower people to do great injustice, atrocity, and evil. If you believe the Bible, you understand that this world is a dangerous place to live. There are people on this planet who are our foes, not friends, no matter what we do.

Human life matters to our God. Our God is the living God; He made us in His image and likeness to have life. As a result, He wants the government (the state) to preserve human life. For example, those who don't believe the Bible seek to decriminalize and defund law and law enforcement, which leads to destruction. The assumption is that when we decriminalize behavior and defund law enforcement, life will get better. But the truth is, life will only get worse. When we dishonor authority, we dishonor God. When honor goes up, blessings come down. When dishonor goes up, cursing comes down.

In addition to civil authority existing to restrain vice, the Church's authority exists to promote virtue. We cannot look to the government for this. The government's laws are broad, and God's laws are narrow. For example, the government tells us not to murder anyone, but Jesus also says we are

ROCKING THE BOAT.

not to assault anyone with our words or in our hearts. The government forbids sexual assault, but Jesus also commands us not to commit adultery with our bodies or in our minds. The expectations for God's people are far narrower and more specific because the moral capacity of a human being with the Holy Spirit is significantly different from that of a fallen person without the Holy Spirit.

As God's people, we should seek not only to honor the government but also to honor God, His laws, and His authority over those of the government. In so doing, even when we disagree, we conduct ourselves in such a way that we're demonstrating moral character. God's people should care about civil laws for crimes and God's laws for sins. This leads to the subject of the state and the sword. The concept of the sword looms large in the Bible. The first person to wield a sword in Scripture was the angel in Genesis 3:24. "[God] drove out the man, and at the east of the Garden of Eden he placed the cherubim and a flaming sword that turned every way to guard the way to the tree of life." There was no sword until there was sin. The last person to wield a sword in Scripture is the Lord Jesus in Revelation 19:15-16: "From his mouth comes a sharp sword with which to strike down the nations, and he will rule them with a rod of iron. He will tread the winepress of the fury of the wrath of God the Almighty. On his robe and on his thigh he has a name written, King of kings and Lord of lords."

Between Genesis and Revelation, God hands out swords to enact justice, to deal with sin, and to protect the sanctity of human life. The sword represents the just taking of human life. Some well-intended Christians have misunderstood the meaning of the sixth commandment: "You shall not murder".[a] In the ancient Hebrew language, there were a multitude of words for the taking of human life. If you took an innocent human life, that was murder. If you took a guilty human life, that was killing. There is a profound difference between murder and killing because one is unjust, and the other is just. The Bible does not say, "Thou shall not kill." It says, "Thou shall not murder." It does not say you cannot take human life. It says you can only take guilty, not innocent, human life.

[a] Exodus 20:13

Romans 13:5-7

Romans 13:5–7 – Therefore one must be in subjection, not only to avoid God's wrath but also for the sake of conscience. For because of this you also pay taxes, for the authorities are ministers of God, attending to this very thing. Pay to all what is owed to them: taxes to whom taxes are owed, revenue to whom revenue is owed, respect to whom respect is owed, honor to whom honor is owed.

The government office people tend to hate the most, no matter the nation, is the one that collects taxes. Government doesn't create wealth; the government takes what people produce. In Mark 12:17, Jesus said, "Render to Caesar the things that are Caesar's, and to God the things that are God's." Taxes are "the things that are Caesar's," and the tithe is "the things that are God's." The tithe is the first 10 percent of our income, which we are supposed to give to God. This act of worship, often called the "firstfruits" in Scripture, is much fairer and more just than taxation. The United States government has a sliding, escalating tax structure. The more a person makes, the higher the percentage they pay. God has a different method. No matter if you are rich or poor, He asks you to give the same percentage. God's economy is always fairer than the economy of this world.

One of the reasons taxes are so frustrating for many people is that we pay for things we like as well as things we do not like. We like roads, infrastructure, and first responder departments. As believers, we dislike godless abortion and public school sex education curricula. The Bible has zero verses about the government's responsibility to educate a child, and Scripture does not support the corrupt, abusive, and godless sex "education" being forced upon children in America's classrooms.

No one enjoys paying taxes, and, as Christians, we should always fight for family, faith, and freedom. If the idea of taxation feels unjust and counterintuitive to our faith, we can look to the example of Jesus and His earthly parents. Mary and Joseph went to Bethlehem, the location of Jesus' birth, because everyone in Israel was told to go back to the man's hometown to register for the census so they could pay taxes. Though they were likely poor, rural teenagers, Jesus' parents set the example before Jesus even entered the world. If you are going to pay your taxes, you really should pay your tithe. You may not be able to avoid funding the things you hate, but you can choose to fund the One you love. Despite all the tax dollars that have been spent in America, the nation is in decline for reasons we will examine in the next chapter.

CHAPTER 3
Why is America a Nation in Decline?

Proverbs 14:34 – Righteousness exalts a nation, but sin is a reproach to any people.

M any Christians are wondering where the United States of America is regarding our place in history. Curiously, there is a book of the Bible called Judges that serves as an interesting historical comparison. The book of Judges covers the first roughly 300 years of the nation of Israel's history.

At the time I am writing this book, the U.S. is around 250 years old, which is roughly the same age Israel was when Samson, the 12th and final judge, began to reign. Curiously, as I am writing, the leading Republican candidate for the presidency is a bit Samsonian – incredibly resilient despite being attacked on all sides with unending energy and strength, a penchant for beautiful but godless women (including prostitutes and porn stars), unable to keep a team unified to work with him, and rarely seen doing religious things like praying but somehow is the hope of God's people.

Prophetically, Jesus said to Samson's parents in Judges 13 that he would be raised up to war against the Philistines over a small piece of land in Israel. Today, as I write, there is a war in Gaza between the Jews (who are descendants of Samson) and the Palestinians (who are likely at least partly descendants of the ancient Philistines that Samson warred against following an invasion and attack on civilians). Judges 16:1 says that 3000 years ago, "Samson went to Gaza..." for war. The Bible tells us not just what happened but what always happens, because it is prophetic.

Everyone Did What Was Right in Their Own Eyes

There are three significant parallels between ancient Israel, as reported in Judges, and modern America.[a]

One, people did not care what was right in God's eyes and only did what was right in their eyes, despite repeated prior warnings:

- Exodus 15:26: ...do that which is right in his eyes...
- Deuteronomy 6:18: ...do what is right and good in the sight of the Lord...
- Deuteronomy 12:25: ...do what is right in the sight of the Lord.
- Deuteronomy 12:28: ...do what is good and right in the sight of the Lord your God.
- Deuteronomy 13:18: ...doing what is right in the sight of the Lord your God.
- Deuteronomy 21:9: ...do what is right in the sight of the Lord.

God also warned His people repeatedly NOT to do what was right in their own eyes. Deuteronomy

[a] I taught from Judges on Deborah, Gideon, and Samson. Visit RealFaith.com to find sermons, transcripts, and study guides for the series.

12:8 says, "You shall not do according to all that we are doing here today, everyone doing whatever is right in his own eyes..." In complete defiance and disobedience, twice in Judges (17:6 and the closing line of 21:25, which is the theme of the entire book), we are told that "everyone did what was right in his own eyes."

In previous generations, Christians spoke of this with the Latin phrase *coram deo*, which means to live in the face of our all-seeing God. In the days of the Judges, the people disobeyed God and had national, political, and spiritual problems as a result. 1 John 2:15-16 says of our demonic world system ruled by Satan: "Do not love the world or the things in the world. If anyone loves the world, the love of the Father is not in him. For all that is in the world – the desires of the flesh and the desires of the eyes and pride of life – is not from the Father but is from the world."

In Samson's life as the last judge, he serves as a painful example of doing that which is right in our eyes instead of God's, which aptly summarizes the Western world.

- Judges 14:1: Samson...saw one of the daughters of the Philistines.
- Judges 14:3: Samson said to his father, "Get her for me, for she is right in my eyes."
- Judges 14:7: ...she was right in Samson's eyes.
- Judges 16:1: Samson...saw a prostitute, and he went in to her.

Later in life, in a tragic plot twist, Samson (who did what was right in his eyes but not what was right in God's eyes) had his eyes gouged out.[a] Judges 16:28 says, "Then Samson called to the Lord and said, 'O Lord God, please remember me

[a] Judges 16:21

25

and please strengthen me only this once, O God, that I may be avenged on the Philistines for my two eyes.'"

Samson was a political leader who did what was right in his eyes, not God's eyes. The Bible makes it clear that he was a man who gambled and drank with pagans, tortured animals, murdered many, broke every command God gave him, and slept with pagan women, including an unblushing trip to a brothel in the middle of the day. Admittedly, Samson would not qualify to be a kids' volunteer in any church, but he was a political judge over Israel longer than any other judge. Today, our politicians are eerily similar. Today, we have phones and other screens that continually tempt us to also do what is right in our eyes and not do what is right in God's eyes. The result is that the generation who invented the selfie, who, for the first time in history, decided we all needed to have a camera that faced us, has decided to do what is right in their own eyes.

Two, things get worse and worse. There is a powerful myth of progressivism, based upon a false evolutionary concept, which states that people are basically good and getting better. Subsequently, this myth says that if we encourage people to feel better about themselves, they will naturally become better people. Morally, the Bible says the exact opposite. People are born with a sin nature imputed from Adam, and, apart from restraining forces like our conscience, painful life consequences, the legal system, police officers, soldiers, and potential death, people would spiral into evil at a rapid rate. Apart from people being saved by Jesus, filled with the restraining and renewing power of the Holy Spirit, and living under the authority of God's Word, they get worse and not better over time. This is plainly stated as a fact for the roughly 300-year history of the book of Judges. Judges 2:19 says, "...they turned back and were more corrupt than their fathers..."

Three, the same demons at work 3000 years ago continue their work today. Judges 2:19-20 continues, "...going after other gods, serving them and bowing down to them. They did not drop any of their practices or their stubborn ways. So the anger of the Lord was kindled..." Judges 3:5-6 goes on to explain this very sin happening that looked like interfaith marriage but was actually spiritual warfare: "So the people of Israel lived among the Canaanites, the Hittites, the Amorites, the Perizzites, the Hivites, and the Jebusites. And their daughters they took to themselves for wives, and their own daughters they gave to their sons, and they served their gods."

These powerful demonic forces are referred to as a "god" or the "gods" throughout Judges.[a] Two of the most prominent demonic counterfeit gods in Judges are Baal and Asherah. He is about power, fame, money, and success, and she is about beauty, lust, pleasure, sex, and seduction. Today, they run most of Western culture in everything from the porn industry to sex trafficking, prostitution, friends with benefits, the abortion industry, adultery, entertainment, and the government. Although we have new people 3000 years later, we are dealing with the same old demons doing the same old things. We will examine all of this in more detail in the chapter on globalism. The issue in both Ancient Israel and the modern West is the same: demonic forces at work result in syncretism that leads to apostasy.

[a] Judges 2:3, 2:11, 2:12, 2:13, 2:17, 2:19, 3:3, 3:6, 3:7, 5:8, 6:10, 6:25-32, 8:33, 9:4, 9:9, 9:27, 10:6, 10:10, 10:13-14, 10:16, 11:24, 16:23-24, 17:5, 18:14, 18:17-18, 18:20, 18:24 6:25, 20:33

Syncretism, Apostasy, and "Christian" Leaders

Syncretism occurs when some of the basic core beliefs of the faith are kept, the rest are discarded, and in their place is some other ideology. Today, for example, in mainline liberal Protestant denominations, the parts of the Bible about doing justice, loving mercy, and caring for others are kept while the holiness and wrath of God, along with repentance of sexual sin (including homosexuality and transgenderism), and belief in Hell are discarded and replaced with progressive politics and universalistic spirituality where all beliefs and behaviors are tolerated and celebrated.

INDEPENDENCE DAY. 1933.

Without repentance, syncretism quickly turns to apostasy.

There's a big difference between someone who is lost and someone who is apostate. Someone who is lost has never professed Christ. Someone who is apostate professed Christ at some point but is no longer practicing their faith. What we're seeing today is a generational apostasy. Often referred to as being "woke," this is the counterfeit of being "born again."

Apostasy is the word that best describes our days and the days of the Judges, when everyone "did what was right in his own eyes" (21:25). An Encyclopedia of Psychology & Counseling says, "Apostasy refers to the process of turning away from Christianity and from one's relationship with God. It is considered an egregious sin (2 Peter 2:20–21), synonymous with falling away from the faith and rebellion."[5] It goes on to say,

> Richard Baxter...one of the great Puritan pastors, discussed some signs of growing apostasy: when sin's delights are continually greater than the pleasures of holiness; when repentance is put off; when legitimate admonitions of others are resisted; when sin becomes easy and conscience offers no argument; and when sin is mentally and verbally defended.[6]

Judges Cycle

The entire backdrop of Judges is divine judgment and sounds a lot like America today. Like us, the ancient Israelites failed to secure their border, so their enemies overtook their nation and consumed their resources, sending the nation into decline. Those who overtook their nation

29

did not care about their God but were pleasing in the bedroom and the boardroom. Rather than having conflict and leading their families, God's men sinfully slept with unbelieving women who were hot like Hell, did business with godless men, and enjoyed a comfortable life. They were like Samson, who was seduced by the sexual double agent Delilah into destruction through indulgence in pleasure, comfort, and ease. In short, their nation was not conquered by force but rather seduced by pleasure. Their nation and ours became soft, starting with the men. Kids who had "believing parents" never heard about God, went to government schools that taught nothing about God, and Judges 2:10 reports, "And there arose another generation after them who did not know the Lord or the work that he had done for Israel."

The sins of Samson, the ancient politician, and the people he led consisted primarily of corrupt sexuality driven by counterfeit spirituality, as in our own day. If there were a book of the Bible that captured the cultural morality of the current Western world, Judges would be a leading candidate. This same pattern in ancient Israel is true in the current Western world:

1. God's people do evil and syncretize with demonic counterfeits.
2. God becomes angry and hands them over to an enemy.
3. God's people cry to Him for help.
4. God raises up leaders who deliver them from their enemies.
5. God's people return to demonic apostasy.

In Judges, by the time God announces the birth of Samson, the nation has tragically run into the final step. They had settled for brutal, sinful lives and were not seeking to repent of their sin or return to their God. Unlike previous scenes in Judges where the people eventually cry out to the Lord for deliverance and He hears and answers their cries, in the days of Samson, one generation after another is silent for four decades. God's people had become worldly, completely settling into their addiction and oppression as they lived and adopted the pagan Philistine lifestyle of sin against God without repentance or remorse. A Biblical journal says,

> Though this is the longest period of time in which Israel was under another nation, there is no record of the Israelites crying out to the Lord for deliverance as they had done in the past. Instead they seem to have been content to exist under foreign domination. Judah, which had begun the fight against the Canaanites (1:1-2), had dropped the goal of conquering the land in favor of a peaceful survival under the Philistines.[7]

The Rise and Fall of Civilizations

The book of Judges reports the decline of a nation over the course of roughly 300 years. With the United States nearing a similar age and experiencing a similar decline – morally, spiritually, and politically – it is interesting to compare the nations. Scottish philosopher Alexander Tytler has studied numerous once-great nations and summarized the reasons behind their decline, noting that the average age of the world's greatest civilizations is around 200 years. His summary is known as the Tytler Cycle, which is summarized in my own words below:

- Step 1: From bondage to spiritual growth because of suffering

- Step 2: From spiritual growth to great courage hardened by suffering
- Step 3: From courage to liberty as evil is defeated
- Step 4: From liberty to abundance and prosperity
- Step 5: From abundance to complacency and indifference
- Step 6: From complacency to apathy and laziness
- Step 7: From apathy to dependence on government
- Step 8: From dependence back to bondage

Our problems today are bigger than the government. A God-sized problem cannot be fixed with a government solution. Christians need to be politically involved, but when many, if not most, churches are woke (or at least soft-woke) and led by pastors afraid of criticism and conflict and willing to compromise at every turn for peace and convenience, two things must happen for a culture and nation to change. One, there must be reformation in the Church. God's people need to be led by courageous, prophetic Bible teachers preaching repentance of sin and a return to pure devotion to God in obedience. Two, there must be revival in the streets. If the Church does not even believe or obey the gospel, there is no one to take it to the streets. As people are saved, filled with the Spirit, repentant of sin and pride, and living under the authority of God's Word, deep change can begin to happen. Until these two steps occur, decline, as we are seeing, is inevitable.

Because the mainline "Christian" denominations, state universities, political system, and most media and social media platforms seem completely rotten to the core, our only hope is that young men become fully devoted followers of Jesus Christ and start new families, new churches, new businesses, new ministries, and new schools. This is a countercultural option for future generations. If we lose the young men, I believe all hope is lost. In the next chapter, we will examine why there must be an immovable line between God and government.

THEY'LL PUSH IT THROUGH WITHOUT HELP FROM ANYBODY—

CHAPTER 4
What are the 2 Kingdoms?

Luke 20:25 – He [Jesus] said to them, "Then render to Caesar the things that are Caesar's, and to God the things that are God's."

During every election cycle, we feel a collective ache for Christ's Kingdom to come. Our world has gone terribly wrong, and everything needs changing. Political candidates step forward to vie for the role of savior, each casting a vision of the heavenly future they promise to bring. Like worshipers, supporters throng to fund campaigns, filled with hope that deliverance will come if their candidate wins.

Some political leaders are better than others. That's just common sense. But no human leader is the King of Kings, because no human king rules with Christ's perfection, justice, truth, and grace. Some nations are better than others, but no kingdom is His Kingdom. No kingdom overcomes sin and the curse fully and forever. Only the Kingdom of King Jesus accomplishes what we ultimately long for and need.

Until Jesus returns with His Kingdom, we are left with nations and politics. "The word *politics* originates from the Latin *politicus* and the Greek *politikos*, both of which mean 'a resident of a city' or 'a citizen.' Politics not only embraces governance but is also used to refer to the tactics, methods, and schemes (sometimes unethical) used in governing."[8]

You Cannot Be Biblical Without Being Political

In one sense, the Bible is largely political. The backdrop of the Bible is that God ruled as King over His Kingdom until there was a "war in heaven."[a] Some of the created angels decided to side with their fellow high-ranking angel Satan, declare war on God, and attempt a coup to overthrow God as King and overtake His Kingdom. The holy angels defeated these demons, who were then cast down to earth. In the opening chapters of Genesis, we see Satan successfully defeat Adam, the father of all mankind, establishing himself as the "god of this world."[b] Jesus humbly came to do battle with Satan, and He never sinned. He died on the cross in our place for our sins, paid our debt to God, released us from demonic control, and ascended back to Heaven, where He sits on His throne in glory as King of Kings and Lord of Lords. On earth, we are living in the Last Days, the final period of human history between Jesus' First Coming to save sinners and His Second Coming to establish His Kingdom dominion over everyone and everything everywhere forever.

Throughout the Scriptures and into our own day, we see the battle between God's Kingdom and earthly governments. The backdrop of the Bible is God's battle for His glory and people against godless governments such as Egypt, Babylon, Persia, and Rome. The long list of enemy nations also includes the Canaanites, Amorites,

[a] Revelation 12:7-9 [b] 2 Corinthians 4:4

36

Girgashites, Hittites, Hivites, Jebusites, and Perizzites.

When pagan governments sought to rule over God's people, prophets were often sent to rebuke pagan kings, something that would have been unheard of in those nations.

> Extensive sections of several of the Old Testament Prophetic Books are addressed not to Israel but to pagan nations. These prophecies show that God also holds unbelieving nations accountable for their actions (see Isaiah 13-23; Jeremiah 46-51; Ezekiel 25-32; Amos 1-2; Obadiah—written to Edom; Jonah—sent to Nineveh; Nahum—written to Nineveh; Habakkuk 2; Zephaniah 2). A number of other passages teach God's sovereignty over the selection and establishment of governmental rulers, including rulers in secular nations. Through Moses, God said to Pharaoh, "For this purpose I have raised you up, to show you my power, so that my name may be proclaimed in all the earth" (Ex. 9:16). God also predicted, through Isaiah, the establishment of Cyrus, king of Persia, about 150 years before his life: [The LORD] says of Cyrus, "He is my shepherd, and he shall fulfill all my purpose." ...Thus says the LORD to his anointed, to Cyrus, whose right hand I have grasped, to subdue nations before him. (Isa. 44:28-45:1).[9][a]

The Bible has a lot to say about God's sovereign rule over nations and rulers.

---

[a] When Isaiah prophesied (about 740-681 B.C.), the Assyrian Empire was dominant in the ancient Near East. But Assyria was defeated by forces of the Babylonian Empire in 612 B.C. Then Babylon fell to the Persians in 539 B.C.

The idea of God's appointment of rulers is expressed in a general way by the psalmist: For not from the east or from the west and not from the wilderness comes lifting up, but it is God who executes judgment, putting down one and lifting up another. (Ps. 75:6–7) Daniel also affirms this about God: "He removes kings and sets up kings" (Dan. 2:21) and "The Most High rules the kingdom of men and gives it to whom he will" (4:25; see also vv. 17, 32). Furthermore, "John the Baptist rebuked Herod 'for all the evil things that Herod had done'" (Luke 3:19). Daniel told Nebuchadnezzar, "Break off your sins by practicing righteousness" (Dan. 4:27). Old Testament history contains many stories of kings who "did what was evil in the sight of the LORD" (1 Kings 11:6). Therefore, we should say that governmental rulers do "good" when they carry out their responsibilities in a just and fair way, following God's principles for government.[10]

In many pagan nations, from the Old Testament to the New Testament and into our present day, there was no separation of Church and state. The King was often considered a god or demigod. This was the case in Egypt (Exodus), explains why King Nebuchadnezzar demanded the entire nation bow down in worship to a golden statue of himself (Daniel), and is why the Roman Empire said, "Caesar is lord."

In contrast, God established the nation of Israel as a theocracy, meaning it is "ruled by God" through a monarchy. Theocracy is a "form of government which acknowledges God alone as the highest political authority, whether or not he is represented by a human ruler such as a king. Thus Deuteronomy 17:14–20 argues that a human king

rules only as one designated for kingship by the Lord."[11]

In a theocracy, there is no clear separation of Church and state. God's laws in the Scriptures are also supposed to be the laws of the nation. For this reason, it can be difficult to draw clear comparisons between the interactions of believers in the Old Testament and Christians living today because these countries are not theocracies.

2 Kingdoms

The Bible makes it clear that our eternal

"citizenship is in heaven."[a] However, until we die or Jesus returns, our residence is temporarily in a nation on earth. The tension for the believer is how to live between these two realities and be politically active for God and good in our nation in honor of His Kingdom. This brings us to the role of Christians in politics.

Believers have always believed in "two kingdoms" based upon the teachings of the Old and New Testaments. Those two kingdoms are the Church and the state. The Church deals with salvation and making people new, and the state deals with restraining evil. The Church is about preparing people for eternity, and the state's only concern is people's lives on earth. The state can never replace the Church, and not everyone in the state is a member of the Church because many do not know and love Jesus Christ as Savior and Lord.

The two kingdoms are on full display in the Old Testament. The priests descended from the line of Levi (Church). The kings descended from the tribe of Judah (state). When King Saul sought to do a priestly act and offer a sacrifice, God punished him, cutting his line off from the kingship.[b] When King Uzziah sought to burn incense on the altar as a priest, God struck him with leprosy.[c]

To use an analogy, think of the Church and the state as two separate lanes on a road. When the state veers into the Church's lane, God gets angry, and things get messy. That is precisely the point of the stories of Kings Saul and Uzziah. They were political leaders who tried to do priestly duties, and God swiftly and severely punished them. When these political leaders veered into the Church lane, God made a public example of them with judgment. Today, we are seeing the state repeatedly veer into

[a] Philippians 3:20 [b] 1 Samuel 13 [c] 2 Chronicles 26:16-21

the Church lane. Examples include trying to force
Christian businesses to make cakes and invitations
for same-sex weddings, forcing Christian employers
to fund the holocaust of abortion, and governments
seizing custody of children from their parents if
they have mental health problems and gender
confusion. When the state veers into the Church
lane, there will be horns honked, some dents, and
the occasional head-on collision if we are to remain
faithful to our God and remain in the lane He has
called us to. Jesus had numerous conflicts with the
Roman government in His day.

> Jesus was inextricably involved in this confusion
> of government. He was attacked at birth (Mt.
> 2:16) as a threat to Herod's throne, and
> denounced in death as a pretender to royal
> power (Jn. 19:21). He was dogged on all sides
> by pressures to avow this goal. The devil's
> advances (Mt. 4:9) were mirrored in popular
> enthusiasm (Jn. 6:15), the obtuse arrogance of
> the disciples (Mt. 16:22f.) and the fears of
> those who precipitated the arrest (Jn. 11:50).
> Faced with such a consensus of misconstruction,
> Jesus generally avoided the claim to kingship,
> but did not conceal it from the disciples (Lk.
> 22:29-30) and in the end owned it publicly (Jn.
> 18:36-37).[12]

Jesus also taught the two kingdoms principle
repeatedly. When the Roman prefect Pontius Pilate
asked if He was plotting a political revolution,
Jesus replied, "My kingdom is not of this world."[a]
Jesus the King rules over all kings, and His
Kingdom reigns over all kingdoms. However, the
Kingdom of our King Jesus has not yet come in

[a] John 18:36

its fullness, and until we see it, we are to pray as He taught us: "Your kingdom come."[a] Jesus' Kingdom has begun its' reign on earth through the preaching of the gospel and the presence of God in the Church, but until He returns, the two kingdoms remain. We read of Jesus in Luke 20:19-25:

> The scribes and the chief priests sought to lay hands on him at that very hour, for they perceived that he had told this parable against them, but they feared the people. So they watched him and sent spies, who pretended to be sincere, that they might catch him in something he said, so as to deliver him up to the authority and jurisdiction of the governor. So they asked him, "Teacher, we know that you speak and teach rightly, and show no partiality, but truly teach the way of God. Is it lawful for us to give tribute to Caesar, or not?" But he perceived their craftiness, and said to them, "Show me a denarius. Whose likeness and inscription does it have?" They said, "Caesar's." He said to them, "Then render to Caesar the things that are Caesar's, and to God the things that are God's."

Here, Jesus clearly taught the two kingdoms principle: that some things belong to the state (Caesar) and others belong to the Kingdom (God).

In the New Testament, there are examples of godly believers involved in the politics of the state.

> Furthermore, the [New Testament] does not specifically forbid Christians to participate in government service—whether in military service

[a] Matthew 6:10

42

or in judicial, executive, or legislative responsibilities. This is shown by the rather large number of converts who held public office without anyone calling them to renounce their position; e.g., the Ethiopian eunuch, Cornelius, Sergius Paulus, the Philippian jailer. Paul's references to "those in Caesar's household" possibly refer to persons holding official status in the government of the Roman empire. Again, this is in keeping with the positions of authority of certain [Old Testament] believers, e.g., Joseph in Egypt, Daniel in Babylon, Mordecai in Persia, Naaman in Syria. The conclusion of most Christians is that they may participate in government as the political situation allows, not only by voting but also by serving as employees or as elected officials. In any case, believers exercise this prerogative as individual Christian citizens and not as representatives of the Church.[13]

5 Kinds of Christian Citizens

Throughout church history, there has generally been a handful of ways that various Christian traditions engage with the state and politics:

1. *Catholic:* The two kingdoms do exist, and the Church is greater while the state is lesser.
2. *Anabaptist:* The two kingdoms do exist; however, the state is evil and part of the world system run by Satan, so Christians in the church should separate from the worldly state by not voting, running for office, or serving in the military.
3. *Calvinist:* The two kingdoms should function more like one kingdom. God gives authority to both the Church and state, and Christians are citizens of both the Church and state.

The ultimate goal of the state is to help the Church Christianize the world. This explains why Calvin held both political and religious roles. Calvin also had a heretic named Servetus executed via capital punishment by the state, which has been a point of great controversy ever since.

4. *Lutheran:* The two kingdoms do exist, and the Christian is a citizen of both the Church and state. The state exists mainly to restrain evil and should not be used to advance the Church, but the Church should rather use the state to protect the freedom to advance the Kingdom through the preaching of the gospel.

5. *Evangelical:* The two kingdoms do exist, and the Church functions somewhere between Calvinist and Lutheran. The Church should advance the Kingdom, the state should protect the Church, and the Church should seek to influence the state to enact godly laws.

No matter which of these five views Christians hold, the Bible makes it clear that before we judge our government, we should first judge our own hearts to ensure we are right with God before trying to change the government.

- Proverbs 24:21: My son, fear the Lord and the king, and do not join with those who do otherwise...
- Ecclesiastes 10:20: Even in your thoughts, do not curse the king, nor in your bedroom curse the rich, for a bird of the air will carry your voice, or some winged creature tell the matter.
- 1 Timothy 2:1-2: First of all, then, I urge that supplications, prayers, intercessions, and thanksgivings be made for all people, for kings and all who are in high positions, that

we may lead a peaceful and quiet life, godly
and dignified in every way.
• Titus 3:1: Remind them to be submissive to
rulers and authorities, to be obedient, to be
ready for every good work...

Theologian Wayne Grudem says,

If Christians are wondering whether it is right
to attempt to bring significant Christian
influence to bear on civil governments and
government leaders, we have encouragement
from many positive examples in the narrative
history of the Bible, including Joseph, Moses,
Daniel, Jeremiah, Nehemiah, Mordecai, and
Esther. We also have as examples the written
prophecies of Isaiah, Ezekiel, Amos, Obadiah,
Jonah, Nahum, Habakkuk, and Zephaniah.
In the New Testament we have the courageous
examples of John the Baptist and the apostle
Paul. Such influences on governments are no
minor examples in obscure portions of the
Bible, but are found in Old Testament history
from Genesis all the way to Esther (the last
historical book), in the canonical writing
prophets from Isaiah to Zephaniah, and in the
New Testament in both the Gospels and Acts.
And those are just the examples of God's
servants bringing significant influence to pagan
kings who gave no allegiance to the God of
Israel or to Jesus in the New Testament
times. If we add to this list the many stories
of Old Testament prophets bringing counsel,
encouragement, and rebuke to the good and
evil kings of Israel, then we would include the
histories of all the kings and the writings of
all the prophets—nearly every book of the Old
Testament. And we could add in several

passages from Psalms and Proverbs that speak of good and evil rulers. Influencing government for good on the basis of the wisdom found in God's words is a theme that runs throughout the entire Bible.[14]

In the next chapter, we will examine the role and influence of Christianity on the founding and flourishing of the United States of America.

GETTING LONESOME

CHAPTER 5
What is the Role of Christianity in American Politics?

Psalm 47:8 – God reigns over the nations; God sits on his holy throne.

Some years ago, I was on a college campus to meet with some students who were new Christians. They had been sharing their newfound faith with non-Christian friends and were getting several questions they did not know the answers to. Since I was their pastor, they invited me to come and meet with their friends and answer their questions about Christianity. The conversation was warm until we got to the issue of politics, and then the students became incensed at the involvement of Christians in politics. One student said, "There is supposed to be freedom from religion," to which I replied, "The opposite is in fact true; there is supposed to be freedom of religion." The students said that Christians had no right to try and influence government and laws toward things like being pro-life and having traditional marriage views because those views were not supposed to leave the Church. They did not mind if Christians had Jesus in their hearts so long as He did not show up anywhere else in the world.

In Which God Do We Trust?

How to live as a Christian, a member of God's Kingdom and Church, and a citizen of the United States is admittedly complicated and has a complex history.

> In the early history of the United States, when the Pilgrims established the Mayflower Compact in 1620, and thereby established a form of self-government, they did so with a strong biblical knowledge influenced by many of the passages and principles of Scripture...They also had vivid memories of oppression by the monarchy in England. As a result, the Mayflower Compact established a government by the consent of the governed, and this would set a pattern for the subsequent colonies and for the United States as a whole in later years. The Pilgrims declared that they were forming a "civil body politik" that would enact "laws" for the general good of the colony, and then they said that to that government "we promise all due submission and obedience."[15]

This was a voluntary submission to a government that they themselves had created. It was not imposed on them by a king or some other conquering force. It was a government set up to function with the consent of the governed – a kind of democracy.

These same principles found fuller expression in the U.S. Declaration of Independence:

> We hold these truths to be self-evident, that all men are created equal, that they are endowed by their Creator with certain unalienable rights, that among these are life, liberty, and

the pursuit of happiness. *That to secure these rights, governments are instituted among men, deriving their just powers from the consent of the governed.*

Although there were some forms of democratic government in local areas in ancient and medieval history (such as ancient Athens), when the United States began as a representative democracy in 1776, it could be called the "American experiment," because there were at that time no other functioning national democracies in the world. But after the founding of the United States, and especially in the 20th century, the number of functioning national democracies grew remarkably. The World Forum on Democracy reports that in 1950, there were 22 democracies accounting for 31 percent of the world population and 21 states with restricted democratic practices accounting for 11.9 percent of the world population. In 2015, electoral democracies represented 125 of the 196 existing countries.[16] Approximately 4.1 billion people live in electoral democracies, or 55.8 percent of the world's population.[17] [18]

6 Godly Principles About Government

As a Christian, there are a few core beliefs from the Bible that help establish a more just government.

One, rights come not from government but rather from God through government. The U.S. Declaration of Independence says that "rights" come from our "Creator" and that "governments" exist "to secure these rights." Simply stated, God is over government, and when people forget that fact, the government seeks to remove and replace God as sovereign. This explains why governments seek to be all-knowing and watch our every move, all-present by putting technology everywhere, and all-powerful by taking away the freedom and power of citizens to centralize it under the ever-encroaching hand of government.

Two, because everyone is a sinner, it is best to separate powers rather than have all power held by one leader or a few leaders. Once Jesus returns, He alone will rightly hold all governing power because He is perfect and without sin and therefore the only Person able to not be corrupted by power. Until His return, a separation of political powers is a safeguard against totalitarian tyranny.

Three, we have a legal system based upon laws because that is the pattern established in

the Scriptures. In many nations, from the ancient world to the present, there are not laws but rather a supreme ruler who acts as a tyrannical god and a law unto themselves. However, as Christianity spread across the Roman Empire, spiritual leaders called bishops were given oversight of various geographic areas, and this included the legal right bestowed by the government to decide legal cases. Eventually, there was a Christian named Justinian who became emperor, and he was largely responsible for establishing a more organized and formalized version of Roman law that helped pave the way for the legal systems in America and Europe today. As historian Rodney Stark notes, "Documents as important as the American Declaration of Independence or the European Charter of Human Rights can therefore be traced back to the ideas of the Christian legal system of Justinian."[19]

Four, the Bible distinguishes between human life and lower levels of animal and plant life. Only men and women are said to bear God's image, unlike anything else in Creation. This God-given distinction helps safeguard the unique sanctity of human life, something that radical animal rights and environmental activists are unable to rightly understand.

Five, because all people equally bear God's image, both men and women, including Christian heterosexuals and non-Christian homosexuals, stand eye-to-eye as human beings and deserve equal protection under the law. As Galatians 3:28 says, "There is neither Jew nor Greek, there is neither slave nor free, there is no male and female..."

Six, the basic framework of the Bible lays the groundwork for a just government. For example, in the 10 Commandments, we are told not to steal, which establishes private property rights extending to forbidding trespassing.[a] They also forbid murder, which establishes the right to life.[b] The New Testament goes on to forbid slave trading[c], along with other crimes that deny human rights established by God. Furthermore, the Bible speaks of peace through military strength[d], equality before the law[e], and the importance of justice.[f]

Was America Founded as a Christian Nation?

In the United States, there is sadly very little understanding among emerging generations about the role of religious commitment in the founding and framing of the nation. Worse still, much of our history is revised according to a Marxist paradigm of the powerful as always evil and the powerless as always victims, so that our heritage is broad brushed as little more than an oppressive collection of racism, sexism, and homophobia, which is how the Father of Lies writes government school curriculum.

The U.S. was not founded with a national religion, but various states did have an official religious commitment. Massachusetts, Connecticut, and New Hampshire were largely Puritan Congregationalists. Virginia, North Carolina, South Carolina, Maryland, and Georgia were largely Anglican. New York allowed each township to determine its' own religion. After the War for Independence, there were 13 states, each with their own preferred religious commitments, and some even had an official state church.[20]

The "Establishment Clause" was established in the First Amendment to the Constitution, saying, when ratified in 1791, "Congress shall make no

[a] Exodus 20:1-17 [b] Ibid [c] 1 Timothy 1:10 [d] 2 Chronicles 26:9-15 [e] Acts 10:34; Exodus 23:6 [f] Jeremiah 23:5; Isaiah 3:13-14; Amos 5:12-15, 7:6

law respecting an establishment of religion, or prohibiting the free exercise thereof; or abridging the freedom of speech, or of the press; or the right of the people peaceably to assemble, and to petition the Government for a redress of grievances." Practically, this established that there would be no federal church over the entire nation and that citizens have a free exercise clause to worship as they please. In 1868's Section One of the 14th Amendment, it says,

> No State shall make or enforce any law which shall abridge the privileges or immunities of citizens of the United States; nor shall any State deprive any person of life, liberty, or property, without due process of law; nor deny to any person within its jurisdiction the equal protection of the laws.

Legal scholars summarize this saying,

> The Fourteenth Amendment has been found to be available to protect a person against governmental action on the part of a state which would without due process deprive him of freedom to disseminate information or freedom of worship. No attempt is here made to formulate a definition of religion or to delineate the concept of separation of church and state, except as it may become pertinent in analysis of judicial opinions.[21]

In 1940, there was a precedent-setting religious liberty case,

> Cantwell v. Connecticut...in which the U.S. Supreme Court on May 20, 1940, ruled unconstitutional a Connecticut statute that

required individuals making door-to-door
religious solicitations to obtain a state license.
The court, in a 9-0 decision, held that the free
exercise clause of the First Amendment applied
to the states through the Fourteenth
Amendment's due process clause, rendering
the states subject to the same restrictions
regarding religion that are placed on
Congress...the court maintained that the First
Amendment prohibited Congress from making
laws regarding the establishment of religion
or preventing free exercise of any religion
and that the Fourteenth Amendment placed
the same prohibitions on state legislatures. The
court explained that the First Amendment gives
citizens both the right to believe and the right
to act. Whereas the first is absolute, the
second, the court observed, is subject to
regulations to protect society. According to
the court, states may make laws regulating
the time, place, and manner of solicitations,
but they may not enact legislation that wholly
prohibits individuals from their right to preach
their religious views. To the extent that the
act required individuals to apply for certificates
to engage in solicitations and were expressly
forbidden to do so without such certificates,
the court reasoned that the law overreached
in regulating religious solicitations. The
Supreme Court also took issue with the fact that
religious solicitors were required to apply
to the secretary of the public welfare council.
The court held that the requirement went too
far because it allowed one person to determine
whether something was a religious cause.
Insofar as the secretary was allowed to
examine facts and use his or her own judgment,
rather than simply issue certificates to anyone

who applied for one, the court concluded that
the process violated the First Amendment as
it applied within the protection of the
Fourteenth Amendment.[22]

In the 1971 case *Lemon vs. Kurtzman,*

the Supreme Court articulated a three-pronged
test to determine whether a particular practice
violates the Establishment Clause. While the
Lemon test is not used by the Court in every
Establishment Clause case, and this test has
been criticized by some justices on the
Court, the Court has often used the Lemon
test to determine Establishment Clause issues.
Lemon was a consolidation of two separate
First Amendment challenges to Pennsylvania
and Rhode Island statutes that provided state
aid to parochial schools. Both statutes provided
aid in the form of salary supplements to
teachers of non-religious subjects at non-public
schools, and the Pennsylvania statute further
provided direct aid to non-public schools in
the form of textbooks and instructional
materials. To determine whether these statutes
violated the Establishment Clause, the Court
applied a three-pronged test based on several
prior Court decisions: "First, the statute must
have a secular purpose; second, its principal or
primary effect must be one that neither
advances nor inhibits religion; finally, the
statute must not foster an excessive government
entanglement with religion." The Court
concluded that both statutes failed the test
because they created the risk of excessive
government entanglement with religious
schools. To ensure the funds provided would
actually be used for non-religious purposes,

the Court reasoned, both statutes would require comprehensive government monitoring and oversight programs. These oversight programs would themselves create excessive government entanglement with religious schools because the government would effectively be required to direct how these schools spent their funds.[23]

In summary,

The First Amendment has two provisions concerning religion: the Establishment Clause and the Free Exercise Clause. The Establishment Clause prohibits the government from "establishing" a religion. The precise definition of "establishment" is unclear. Historically, it meant prohibiting state-sponsored churches, such as the Church of England. Today, what constitutes an "establishment of religion" is often governed under the three-part test set forth by the U.S. Supreme Court in Lemon v. Kurtzman, 403 U.S. 602 (1971). Under the "Lemon" test, government can assist religion only if (1) the primary purpose of the assistance is secular, (2) the assistance must neither promote nor inhibit religion, and (3) there is no excessive entanglement between church and state. The Free Exercise Clause protects citizens' right to practice their religion as they please, so long as the practice does not run afoul of a "public morals" or a "compelling" governmental interest.[24]

What is the "Wall of Separation"?

Those who oppose religious people and organizations being involved in government and law will frequently use the phrase "wall of separation." The idea is that there should be a sort of impermeable wall that keeps religion from influencing government, or a separation of Church and state. The phrase is so well known that some may wonder if it is, in fact, part of any national founding U.S. documents. No, it comes from Thomas Jefferson. In fact, Jefferson was in France when the U.S. Constitution was drafted and not a member of Congress when the First Amendment was passed. This phrase likely came from an address to the Danbury Baptists in 1802, 13 years after the First Amendment passed and 11 years after ratification. Therefore, it is not the definitive interpretation of the First Amendment and was largely intended to keep the government out of the Church, and not the other way around.

On January 1, 1802, President Thomas Jefferson wrote to the Baptist Association of Danbury, Connecticut. For more than a year, it had been actively petitioning against laws that privileged the state faith: Congregationalism. The association appealed to the president for support, calling religion "at all times and places a Matter between God and Individuals" and stating that no one should "suffer in Name, person or effects on account of his religious Opinions." Even though the Bill of Rights had been in effect for a decade, the First Amendment's prohibition of religious establishment was understood to apply only to the federal government. In fact Congregationalists in New England had a standing order for civil authorities to punish "idolatry, blasphemy, heresy, venting corrupt and pernicious opinions." The Dissenters' Petition, as it became known, asked the state legislature to abolish all regulations that interfered with "the natural rights of freemen" or "the sacred rights of conscience." Baptists deeply objected to paying taxes to support Congregational churches. They reminded the president that the few religious privileges they enjoyed were regarded as "favors granted" by the state government, not as "inalienable rights." In his response Jefferson agreed "that religion is a matter which lies solely between man & his god, that he owes account to none other for his faith or his worship, that the legitimate powers of government reach actions only and not opinions." It was a familiar argument he had made earlier in his Virginia Statute of Religious Freedom. To the Baptists Jefferson went on to reference the First Amendment on freedom of religion—which, he explained, built "a wall of separation between Church & State."[25]

The distinction between the Church and state is necessary to protect the Church from becoming weaponized by the government to do evil in the name of God. Any church run by the state cannot fight for the Bible, which we will examine next.

CHAPTER 6
What Happens to Churches That Won't Fight for the Bible?

Jude 1:3 – ...contend for the faith that was once for all delivered to the saints.

As a young senior pastor in my mid-20's, our ministry was comprised of mainly broke college students desperately needing a place to meet for our Sunday night service. There was a beautiful old cathedral near the university that had only a handful of old people attend on Sunday mornings and was vacant the rest of the week. So, I met with the pastor, asking her if we could rent the building on Sunday nights. After multiple meetings together, she brought the request to the board overseeing the church and called me to hear the answer as we sat in her office. I was overjoyed when she said we had been approved to rent the building and then completely devastated when she said there was one more question I needed to answer: "Do you still believe in Paul?" I was dumbfounded. "The Paul in the Bible who wrote roughly half the books of the New Testament and is featured in the book of Acts?" I asked. "Yes, that Paul," she said. I said, "Well, yes, I believe in the writings of Paul that are in the Bible." She laughed, saying, "Well, you shouldn't believe in Paul because he's a sexist, misogynist, bigoted homophobe and should have never gotten into the Bible! We cannot rent the building to anyone who believes in Paul." So, I got up and went home, shaking my head as a new Christian who was shocked to believe that some pastors don't even believe in the Bible.

In every generation, there is a war between the Word and the world. The Word of God stands against the world and calls the world to repentance of sin and a renewing of the mind. To remain a faithful Christian in this world requires a deep commitment to the entirety of God's perfect and true Word. This is especially necessary in our negative world, as the cultural forces at work outside of the Church are constantly at war against Christ and His Church. A Christian must not give up their biblical convictions for some political or cultural gain, no matter how great the payoff might be.

THE WORD VS. THE WORLD

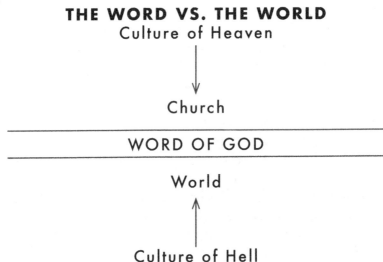

Culture of Heaven

Church

WORD OF GOD

World

Culture of Hell

There is coming a day, perhaps soon, when every nation and culture will disappear and there will only be two cultures remaining: Heaven and Hell. Today, we live in the middle, and the decisions we make every day either invite Heaven down into our lives or pull Hell up into our lives.

Heaven Down or Hell Up?

According to the Scriptures, the Church is supposed to be the place where the culture of Heaven comes down to be with God's people. This is typified in Scripture when the glory of God comes down, Jesus Christ comes down, the Word of God comes down, and the Holy Spirit descends. God's people invite Heaven down when they do such things as repent of sin, obey the Word of God, pray, worship, and seek to live under the Lordship of Jesus Christ by the power of the Holy Spirit. Those who live in this place are living in the place that God blesses.

Conversely, the world is where we find rebellion against God and pulling up the culture of Hell. In our world, everything from lies to pride, perversion, greed, coveting, lawlessness, murder, stealing, and other sins are just the beginning of attitudes and actions that pull Hell up.

Between the Church (culture of Heaven) and the world (culture of Hell) is the Word of God. The Word of God is the dividing line between the Church and the world. The war is always between the Word and the world. The world will never accept the Word of God because it despises the Son of God and is devoid of the Spirit of God. Without the Holy Spirit made possible by a saving relationship with Jesus Christ, the Word of God is foolish and offensive, as the Apostle Paul plainly states.

Because the government is part of the world system, there will always be pressure on the Church to surrender beliefs and behaviors to the state so that the line between the two kingdoms is erased. This begins with a continual movement of the lines where the Word of God causes division between the Church and the world. In our day, this would include the intense demonic pressure from the culture and government for the Church to move the lines drawn by Scripture about binary genders (male and female), marriage only for one man and one woman, and sex solely for heterosexual married couples. Intensifying this pressure are personal relationships, as Christians have loving, close relationships with people who are pressuring them to be accepted without repenting of sin. The pressure is always one way: to move the line south.

To use another analogy, the relationship between the two kingdoms – Church and state – is supposed to be like boating. In boating, the goal is to have the boat in the water but not let the water enter the boat. If you are in a boat at sea and it starts to take on water, you have a crisis on your hands.

Contending for the Faith

The world is like a tumultuous ocean, and the Church is supposed to be like a boat passing through that sea, picking up people who are adrift and rescuing them by pulling them into the boat. When the world starts to flood into the Church, there is a crisis.

This is precisely the backdrop of the book of Jude. Having watched his big brother, Jesus Christ, die for sinners, rise from death, and return to Heaven, Jude was part of the first days of the early Church. Some years later, the zeal of the first Christians began to wane, and new generations of Christians were starting to fill the Church up with the world, which created a crisis that threatened to

sink the Church altogether.

If you can imagine a crew on a boat at sea, many miles away from the shore, bailing water and patching holes, frantically hoping to prevent the brutal sinking of everyone onboard, you can imagine the backdrop for the sense of urgency that Jude writes with. The same worldly waters that were leaking into the ark of the Church in Jude's day continue to leak into the Church in our day: prideful rejection of godly authority, spirituality without the Holy Spirit, sexual sin of every sort propelled by gender confusion, and a celebration of pleasure in most any and every form. The timeless truths in Jude are exactly what we need in our truthless times. When fake "Christians" compromise, they're likely perverting the grace of God into a celebration of sexual sin, gender confusion, and rebellion against the sexual biblical guardrails put in place by our "Master and Lord, Jesus Christ."

The theme of Jude is found in one word, "contend." It means "to exert intense effort... When used in athletic imagery...[it refers to] the one against whom one is contending...the effort expended by the subject in a noble cause...[and the] ideal of dedication to the welfare of the larger group."[26] The word "contend"

> was commonly used in connection with the Greek stadium to denote a strenuous struggle to overcome an opponent, as in a wrestling match. It was also more generally about any conflict, contest, debate, or lawsuit. Involved is the thought of the expenditure of all one's energy in order to prevail. Here, as often, the verb is used metaphorically to denote a spiritual conflict in which believers are engaged.[27]

To contend is about having conflict in a negative world, "the force of the compound verb as 'to fight, standing upon a thing which is assaulted and which the adversary desires to take away, and it is to fight so as to defend it, and to retain it.'"[28]

This language of spiritual warfare, with Christians constantly needing to fight against worldly cultural forces seeking to invade and implode the Church, requires a vigilance that does not take a season off or ever surrender. Every day, the Enemy of God and His people will be on the attack, often through a godless government. There is no such thing as stasis in the Christian life. Every day, we are going forward or backward in our walk with Jesus, and we must contend. "The present tense indicates that such a defense of the faith is a continuing duty for believers."[29]

Jude uses very strong language to denounce these apostate wolves with words of war, saying, "certain people have crept in unnoticed who long ago were designated for this condemnation, ungodly people, who pervert the grace of our God into sensuality and deny our only Master and Lord, Jesus Christ." Like the evildoers of the Old Testament, they will be "destroyed" because they "did not believe." Their hellish fate is "eternal chains under gloomy darkness until the judgment of the great day – just as Sodom and Gomorrah." Because of their "sexual immorality," having "pursued unnatural desire," their fate is "a punishment of eternal fire." In demonic delusion, "these people also, relying on their dreams, defile the flesh, reject authority, and blaspheme the glorious ones." Because "these people blaspheme," they will be "destroyed" for acting like "unreasoning animals." With a curse, Jude says,

> Woe to them! For they walked in the way of Cain and abandoned themselves for the sake of gain...These are blemishes...as they feast with you without fear, looking after themselves; waterless clouds, swept along by winds; fruitless trees in late autumn, twice dead, uprooted; wild waves of the sea, casting up the foam of their own shame; wandering stars, for whom the gloom of utter darkness has been reserved forever.

Facing "judgment," these "ungodly" people have done "deeds of ungodliness," acting in an "ungodly way" as "ungodly sinners," having said and done "harsh things." In our day when Christianity has been repackaged as a safe-for-the-whole-family series of only positive, uplifting, trite self-help insights, we have forgotten that the Bible is for and against beliefs and behaviors in the starkest of language, and choosing between the two is an act of spiritual warfare.

Pulling no punches, Jude adds, "These are grumblers, malcontents, following their own sinful desires; they are loud-mouthed boasters showing favoritism to gain advantage." These "scoffers, following their ungodly passions...cause divisions, worldly people devoid of the Spirit." Being a faithful Christian in a negative world will test your nerve.

> He [Jude] wrote to "exhort" them (Jude 3). In the Greek language, this word was used to describe a general giving orders to the army; hence the atmosphere of this letter is "military." Jude had started to write a quiet devotional letter about salvation, but the Spirit led him to put down his harp and sound the trumpet! The Epistle of Jude is a call to arms.[30]

When Jude admonishes Christians to "contend for the faith that was once for all delivered to the saints," he is referring to a fixed teaching about the gospel of Jesus Christ that is unchanging. The gospel of Jesus Christ is about repentance of sin and faith in His sinless life, substitutionary death, bodily Resurrection, rule over all our lives as Lord, and coming again to judge the living and the dead with sentencing to Heaven or Hell forever. The gospel has the power of God, and to divert from or dilute the gospel is to dishonor God and diminish good for people. No generation or government has the right to make any edits to the Word of God, and every generation and government will be judged by how faithfully they hand off what has been handed to them. The Christian commitment to contending means that there will inevitably be conflicts with the government. Those naïve Christians and pastors who declare that they avoid political issues now find themselves pressed to deal with governments that are seeking to mutilate the genitalia of healthy children with mental health problems, usurp parental authority, and brainwash emerging generations with cultural Marxism and demonic ideology in government schools. In a negative world, the Church has to contend with the state when the state refuses to stay in its' lane and makes everything political.

Contending Against Godless Government

In the negative world, the Church has five vital roles to fill.

One, the Church should serve as a voice of godly authority, reminding the government that it is not God and has limits to its' authority.

Two, the Church should serve a prophetic function, calling everyone to repent of sin, no matter what their political affiliation may be. If our highest commitment is to the gospel of Jesus Christ, the Church cannot and must not ignore sin just because sinners happen to be on their side of the political fight.

> The church should play what can be called a prophetic role in society. This involves dissociating itself from the ideologies and crusades of the state. This means that while the church must obey the state (and even be patriotic), it must be careful not to see its major role as legitimizing the state. When the church becomes too wrapped up in defending the state, it loses its ability to speak for God

against the evils of the state.[31]

Three, the church should seek to set an example for the state with ethical and godly conduct in obedience to God. Of course, this will be met with false accusations and slander from the world against the Church, but this is exactly what the New Testament repeatedly predicts will occur.

Four, because the state is continuously being pulled toward being degenerate and totalitarian, the Church must continuously push back against these tendencies in lawful ways such as protest, legal recourse, and political involvement. "The church should, then, function prophetically to point out evils when they arise and call the state back to God. In American history the role of the church in combating slavery is a prime example of the church playing this prophetic role."[32]

Five, the Church must remain firstly committed to the gospel of Jesus Christ, calling everyone to repentance of sin and life under His sovereign lordship. If the Church fails in this task, the entirety of a culture loses its God-consciousness, which leads to tyranny and terror. In his Templeton Prize address, Aleksandr Solzhenitsyn said: "Over half a century ago, while I was still a child, I recall hearing a number of older people offer the following explanation for the great disasters that had befallen Russia: 'Men have forgotten God; that's why all this has happened.'"[33]

Now that we've looked at how the Church must contend for the gospel and the truth of God's Word, in the next chapter, we'll look at a Christian's view of nationalism and globalism.

CHAPTER 7
Should a Christian Be a Nationalist or a Globalist?

Genesis 11:1,4-6 – Now the whole earth had one language and the same words...Then they said, "Come, let us build ourselves a city and a tower with its top in the heavens, and let us make a name for ourselves, lest we be dispersed over the face of the whole earth." And the Lord said, "Behold, they are one people, and they have all one language, and this is only the beginning of what they will do. And nothing that they propose to do will now be impossible for them..."

Christian nationalism is the current dog whistle for attacking patriotic believers. There is a smear campaign from Left-leaning media to portray people of faith who love their nation as hateful of other nations and, by default, racist. Admittedly, every movement has its lunatic fringe, and this is true on the fringes of both the political Left and Right. However, in this chapter, we will deal with the role of Christianity in America and also examine the Bible to see if Christians should be nationalists or globalists. For starters, America is founded on the belief that above the state is God, that rights for citizens come from God, and that the government is accountable to God for securing and preserving those rights.

Endowed By Their Creator?

The Preamble to the Declaration of Independence from July 4, 1776, says, "We hold these truths to be self-evident, that all men are created equal, that they are endowed by their Creator with certain unalienable Rights, that among these are Life, Liberty and the pursuit of Happiness."

This begs the question, "Who is the God that is our Creator" from whom we derive our "unalienable rights"? Roughly 250 years ago, what was the intended meaning of those who penned these words? Were they thinking of Islam and the possibility that Allah is our Creator and the source of our rights as revealed in the Koran, like the current Islamic neighborhoods in Detroit operating apart from American laws? Were they thinking that our rights could be found in the Marxist curriculum of social science departments, drag queen story hours for kids at the local library, or on the protest signs at Black Lives Matter riots? Were they thinking that the God who gives laws and rights was, in fact, the pantheon of gods and goddesses found in Hinduism?

Admittedly, not all of our Founding Fathers were Christians. Some were deists, and others had religious commitments that are about as clear as fog. However, the role of Christianity as the dominant religious influence in American history is without question. From 1620, when the pilgrims landed, until 1837, virtually all American education was private and Christian. The pastors in the colonies were often the most educated men and led both the intellectual and spiritual lives of the people. In Puritan New England, the first schools

70

(known as common schools) were distinctively Christian. Soon, tax monies were raised to support these schools, and the first public schools in the United States were Christian and remained that way for 217 years. In higher education, nearly every one of the first 123 American colleges and universities founded in the United States was of Christian origins, including Yale, William and Mary, Brown, Princeton, NYU, and Northwestern. Harvard was started by a donation of money and books by Rev. John Harvard. Dartmouth was founded to train missionaries to the Native Americans.

The inauguration of our first president, George Washington, included his getting on his knees to kiss the Bible before leading the Senate and House of Representatives to an Episcopal church for a two-hour worship service. At the very least, the

Founding Fathers were greatly influenced by the Bible, even if they were not all Christians. In fact, 34 percent of all the Founding Fathers' citations in books, pamphlets, articles, and other works were from the Bible.[34]

For those of us who live in America, we should humbly thank God every day that we do enjoy some freedoms that would not have otherwise been granted to us, apart from the influence of Jesus and Christianity on the framework of our nation. For example, in the United States, the fight against slavery was led, in large part, by Christians. This included President Abraham Lincoln, who is widely regarded as perhaps the most important American to fight against slavery and did so because of his Christian convictions. In the fight for civil rights, Martin Luther King, Jr. was a pastor who chose a nonviolent path based upon the example of Jesus Christ, and his base of support came largely from primarily black churches, where the struggle for freedom was preached about in the context of the Exodus story in the Old Testament. To this day, many largely black churches are very politically involved, but you curiously never hear anything negative about black Christian nationalism.

The truth is that every person comes to their politics with their own preferences. Every religious person, along with atheists, agnostics, and deists, believes that their way of viewing the world is helpful in informing their political beliefs. Why is it that the media is so hostile to the Christian faith and so reticent to denounce other faiths? Perhaps it is because many Christians are Republicans and, according to one survey, only 3.4% of journalists are Republicans.[35]

Should a Christian be a Nationalist or a Globalist?

Two competing political ideologies are nationalism and globalism. Globalism manifests itself in many ways including the following two: 1) when a nation sends its troops to fight wars for other nations overseas, or involves a nation in battles not near their borders and 2) when a nation does not secure its borders and allows people from other nations to enter their nation illegally, regardless of their intent.

The first biblical case study in globalism was the city and Tower of Babel in Genesis 10-11. Genesis 10 opens with a lengthy genealogy of people who will be important for the rest of the book. Genesis is basically written in chronological order, with chapters 10-11 being the primary inversion, as Moses' intent is to establish the nations that were scattered out from Babel to best frame the story theologically. The genealogy breaks down into the descendants of Noah's three sons – Ham, Shem, and Japheth – from whom the Egyptians descended.

Throughout Genesis, the concept of going east corresponds to getting farther and farther from God. For example, when Adam and Eve were cast out of the Garden, they went eastward (3:24), as did Cain (4:16). When people go eastward in Genesis, they are walking away from God (typified by Eden and the Promised Land) and into ruin, as places such as Sodom and Babylon lie eastward. This is the backdrop of the Babel story in the Bible: people running away from God.

The people settled in Shinar to create a city (Babylon) and a tower (the Tower of Babel). Using the same language God used for creation, the people said, "Let us make" (referring to their name and reputation). Here we see where the cultural myth of evolution finds its allure. People made great technological progress. They could build a city, but they didn't love God. And the truth is, unless we meet the Lord and receive a new heart, a new nature, and new desires, the only thing we use new technology for is greater evil.

The Tower of Babel would have been the world's first skyscraper. Babylon (also referred to as Babel) is near modern-day Baghdad. The focus of the story is simply not on the building of a tower but rather on the building of a city to house a secular society as a counterfeit of the New Jerusalem that Jesus will bring as headquarters for the New Earth. Their hope was a unified people who would not be scattered but would, apart from God's covenant and blessing, live for themselves by themselves – Heaven on earth without God – the very same counterfeit utopian vision given by Marxism today.

While some have doubted the story of Babel, it has been proven as fact. In 1899, the German archaeologist Robert Koldewey began an 18-year excavation of the mud-brick ancient ruins that are widely believed to be the "ziggurat" Tower of Babel.[36]

God rightly viewed this centralization of power in the hands of proud sinners apart from Him as a dangerous thing. He saved them from themselves and saved others from the potential abuses of power by simply scattering them and confusing their languages. Ironically, this scattering of people and confusion of languages were two of the primary things these people were seeking to prevent from happening in the first place.

So, God's answer is nationalism, not globalism. Satan wants globalism. God's plan was for nations with borders and languages. Love your nation, seek the prosperity and well-being of your nation, and want good for your neighbor and everyone else. And so, we should be nationalists, love our nation, and even be patriotic while praying, "Thy kingdom come, thy will be done, on earth as it is in heaven."[a] The goal is that one day, all of the nations will cease, and the Kingdom of God will come with the Lord Jesus Christ. There will only be globalism when Jesus returns. Revelation 7:9 says, "...I looked, and behold, a great multitude that no one could number, from every nation, from all tribes and peoples and languages, standing before the throne and before the Lamb [worshiping King Jesus]..."

The name Babel, or Babylon, is humorously akin to our English word "babble," which is what their communication sounded like once God confused their language. Beautifully, on the day of Pentecost in Acts 2, through the power of the Holy Spirit, the spiritual gift of tongues temporarily reversed this division as people who were saved from different nations and languages were supernaturally enabled to hear the gospel and worship God despite their language barriers.

The point of Babel and Pentecost is that the hope for our sin problem is not to be found in proud globalism between nations, nationalism for our people, technological advancement, or the working together of unrepentant sinners but rather in the miraculous power of the Holy Spirit. Rather than drowning the sinners as He had in the Flood, God graciously saved them from themselves and simply scattered them, confusing their language to force them to live as He intended – scattering and filling the earth.[b] Subsequently, these scattered people become the nations listed in Genesis 10,

[a] Matthew 6:10 [b] Genesis 1:28

which the Church is later sent to reach with the
good news of the gospel of Jesus Christ in Acts 1:8.
While Christians are not supposed to be globalists,
we are called by God to global missions – reaching
the nations with the good news of the gospel
of Jesus Christ so that a faithful church exists
everywhere as an outpost for the Kingdom of God.

Today, technology and travel are bringing
people and their languages together like no time
in history since Genesis 11. We have seen the
beginnings of globalism. During World War II,
there were global alliances between the Axis
powers (Italy, Japan, and Germany) and Allied
powers (Soviet Union, United States, British
Empire, Poland, France, and the United Kingdom).
Today, the United Nations Security Council and

NATO (North Atlantic Treaty Organization) exhibit versions of globalism. Regional trade deals such as the European Union and North American Free Trade Agreement are also versions of globalism. Financially, the World Bank, International Monetary Fund, and cryptocurrency are attempts at degrees of globalism. Technology and travel are also making the world smaller than ever, pulling nations together into one global collective.

> The G-7, which includes Canada, France, Germany, Italy, Japan, the United Kingdom and the United States, has met regularly since the mid-1980s at the finance minister and central bank governor level. The G-20 has also met regularly since 1999 at the finance minister and central bank governor level. In 2008, the G-20 country leaders began meeting regularly to address the global financial crisis and in 2009 the G-20 was elevated to the premier international economic forum. The members of the G-20 are: Argentina, Australia, Brazil, Canada, China, France, Germany, India, Indonesia, Italy, Japan, Mexico, Russia, Saudi Arabia, South Africa, South Korea, Turkey, the U.K. and the U.S., as well as the European Union, represented by the rotating council presidency and the European Central Bank.[37]

There are also rumblings that the World Health Organization is seeking to impose the equivalent of a global government over all nations if a new "pandemic" hits. If this occurs, nations, including the U.S., will have non-elected non-Americans exercising unprecedented authority.[38] These kinds of efforts at globalism are signs of the End Times, which we will examine next.

CHAPTER 8
How is Globalism a Prophetic Sign of the End Times?

Zechariah 14:2-4 — ...I will gather all the nations against Jerusalem to battle, and the city shall be taken and the houses plundered and the women raped. Half of the city shall go out into exile, but the rest of the people shall not be cut off from the city. Then the Lord will go out and fight against those nations as when he fights on a day of battle. On that day his feet shall stand on the Mount of Olives that lies before Jerusalem on the east, and the Mount of Olives shall be split in two...

Whereas the God of the Bible supports nationalism, it is godlessness that supports globalism. Based upon the progressive myths that people are inherently good, and mankind is evolving into ever-increasing levels of superiority over prior primitive generations, the predominant worldview today is the vision of the Humanist Manifesto II from 1973, which says,

> humans are responsible for what we are or will become. No deity will save us; we must save ourselves...The ultimate goal should be the fulfillment of the potential for growth in each human personality – not for the favored few,

but for all of humankind. Only a shared world and global measures will suffice...We deplore the division of humankind on nationalistic grounds. We have reached a turning point in human history where the best option is to transcend the limits of national sovereignty and to move toward the building of a world community in which all sectors of the human family can participate. Thus we look to the development of a system of world law and a world order based upon transnational federal government. This would appreciate cultural pluralism and diversity...For the first time in human history, no part of humankind can be isolated from any other. Each person's future is in some way linked to all. We thus reaffirm a commitment to the building of world community, at the same time recognizing that this commits us to some hard choices...At the present juncture of history, commitment to all humankind is the highest commitment of which we are capable; it transcends the narrow allegiances of church, state, party, class, or race in moving toward a wider vision of human potentiality. What more daring a goal for humankind than for each person to become, in ideal as well as practice, a citizen of a world community.[39]

The Antichrist Loves Globalism

The globalist agenda is, by its own admission, godless. According to many Christians' reading of the Bible, the rise of a one-world global government is an End Times sign that the Second Coming of Jesus Christ is very near.

If so, we are living in the Last Days.

If you have the Holy Spirit and have walked

with Jesus, you can see it in the world and sense it in your soul. Younger believers may not fully understand how dark our world has become because it was the world they were born into. However, if you ask any older saint who has been walking with the Lord for many decades, they will tell you that what is celebrated in the world and tolerated in the Church is so obviously dark, diabolical, and demonic that they are shocked and appalled. Older saints could have never fathomed such things as the denial of binary gender categories and ensuing craziness that includes boys in girls' locker rooms after competing in female sports, genital mutilation of children in the name of "care," sexualization of minors, hatred of the Bible, eroding of freedom due to the encroaching of government in seemingly every corner of culture, open socialistic support, legalization of hard drugs, dishonor of marriage, and celebration of abortion and political candidates running on these issues as virtues.

Even non-Christians can sense that we are living in the End Times of the Last Days. A recent Pew Research Center survey says,

In the United States, 39% of adults say they believe "we are living in the end Times"... Christians are divided on this question, with 47% saying we are living in the end times, including majorities in the historically Black (76%) and evangelical (63%) Protestant traditions. Viewed more broadly, the share of Protestants who say we are living in the end times is greater than the corresponding share among Catholics (55% vs. 27%)...The survey also explored Americans' views about a core tenet of Christianity: the belief that Jesus will eventually return to Earth, in what is often called the "second coming." When asked if Jesus "will return to Earth someday," more than half of all U.S. adults (55%), including three-quarters of Christians, say this will happen. Protestants in the evangelical (92%) and historically Black (86%) traditions are more likely than other Christians to say there will eventually be a second coming of Jesus. Respondents who said they believe Jesus will return to Earth were also asked how certain they are that this will happen during their lifetime. One-in-ten Americans say they believe the second coming of Jesus will definitely or probably occur during their lifetime, 27% are not sure if Jesus will return in their lifetime...[40]

In the Bible, the End Times, or "Last Days"[a] are also referred to as the "last time"[b], and "last hour."[c] The "Last Days" refers to the period of time between Jesus' First Coming to save sinners and His Second Coming to join Heaven and Earth into the eternal Kingdom of God, with people sentenced to Heaven and Hell forever. The Bible refers to Jesus' Second Coming, which brings the "Last Days" to a close and ushers in the resurrection of the dead and eternal state as the "Day of the Lord" or simply "the Day."[d] Thus far, the "Last Days" have been roughly two thousand years. We are living in the time between the times, in the middle of history. Looking back, we can see God's prophecies regarding the First Coming of our Lord having been fulfilled, and we can look forward to God fulfilling the remaining prophecies about the Second and Final Coming of our Lord.

[a] John 6:39-40; Acts 2:17-18; Hebrews 1:1-2 [b] 1 Peter 1:5, 1:20; Jude 18 [c] 1 John 2:18 [d] see, e.g., Isaiah 2:12-22; Ezekiel 13:5; Joel 1:15; 2:1,11; Amos 5:18-24; Zephaniah 1:7,14-15

The Satanic Six

The Bible makes it clear that these "Last Days" will be marked by six increased evil and demonic activities:

1. An increase in stress, anxiety, and mental illness.[a]
2. An increase in scoffers who mock the Bible and those who believe it.[b]
3. An increase in mockers of Christian morality who encourage pleasure, especially sexual sin.[c]
4. An increasing love for false teachers and corresponding hatred for Bible preachers.[d]
5. An increase in people who are anti-Christ, leading a massive counterfeit "Christian" apostasy, which paves the way for the Antichrist.[e]
6. An increase in wealth, comfort, and a sense that God is not needed for a successful life or concern for eternity.[f]

Writing to Bishop Creighton in 1887, Lord Acton made the now famous statement, "Power tends to corrupt and absolute power corrupts absolutely."[41]

Until Jesus returns, the Antichrist will be pushing for globalism in every generation so that he can arise to rule and reign on earth. Throughout human history, there has been a parade of people who seem to be the embodiment of evil, proving this very tragic truth: centralized political power leads to demonically empowered dictators who bring death and destruction.[42]

Khmer Rouge regime leader Pol Pot brought genocide to Cambodia from 1975 to 1979. It is estimated that anywhere from 3.5 to 5 million

[a] 2 Timothy 3:1 [b] 2 Peter 3:3 [c] Jude 18 [d] 2 Timothy 4:1-4 [e] 1 John 2:18-19 [f] James 5:5

people died in a failed attempt at agrarian socialism based upon the failed communist teachings of Stalinism and Maoism, so that 25% of the nation's population was murdered in some form or fashion by their government.

Ranavalona I of Madagascar had a 13-year reign of terror (1829-1842). Half the citizens of Madagascar died as the total population fell from 5 to 2.5 million citizens across the island.

The Nazi holocaust (1939-1945) took the lives of some 17 million people. Adolf Hitler looked a lot like the Bible's depiction of the Antichrist – worshiped like a god with seemingly supernatural power trying to rule the earth with evil force.

Joseph Stalin's rule (1922-1953) included murder, famine, slavery, and massacres that took

the lives of an estimated 15 million people at minimum, with some estimates being much higher.

Lastly, Chinese dictator Mao Zedong (1946-1976) imposed slave labor, killed political dissidents, exterminated entire classes of people, and let 15 million people starve to death, with some estimates saying he is responsible for the deaths of upwards of 70 million people.

To be anti-Christ is to seek to remove Christ as Lord and replace Christ with another lord. 2 Thessalonians 2:4 says he "exalts himself against every so-called god or object of worship, so that he takes his seat in the Temple of God, proclaiming himself to be God." Throughout history, anti-Christ leaders have been filled with demonic power to do anti-ministry.[43]

2 John 1:7 says that the parade of anti-Christs throughout history will culminate in the coming of the Antichrist at the end of history: "For many deceivers have gone out into the world, those who do not confess the coming of Jesus Christ in the flesh. Such a one is the deceiver and the antichrist."

In 2 Thessalonians 2:1-2, Paul teaches about the "man of lawlessness." Before Jesus returns, this fully Satanic, possessed world leader will rise up, seeking to rule the earth in place of Christ: "The coming of the lawless one is by the activity of Satan with all power and false signs and wonders, and with all wicked deception for those who are perishing, because they refused to love the truth and so be saved."

Combining politics, religion, and celebrity status, people from the nations of the earth will worship the Antichrist as the globalist hope of the planet and love him because he preaches celebration of sin instead of repentance of sin to those who take "pleasure in unrighteousness."[a]

Where is history going? The progressive myth that people are good and civilizations improve over time is a lie. The storyline of the Bible is that people are sinners, the world is cursed, Satan and demons are real, and evildoers are everywhere. "To convince the Thessalonians that the Day of the Lord had not yet arrived, in 2 Thess 2:1–12 Paul asserts that two events must first occur: the arrival of the man of lawlessness and 'the rebellion' (hē apostasia). Typically translated as 'rebellion' or 'apostasy' in English..."[44]

Knowing that the spirit of anti-Christ is at work in our world until Jesus comes to forever defeat it helps us to understand why life is hard and politics is war, even though God is good, and assures us that the end is coming, and the new eternity is certain.

> ...that day will not come, unless the rebellion comes first, and the man of lawlessness is revealed, the son of destruction, who opposes and exalts himself against every so-called god or object of worship, so that he takes his seat in the temple of God, proclaiming himself to be God...And you know what is restraining him now so that he may be revealed in his time. For the mystery of lawlessness is already at work. Only he who now restrains it will do so until he is out of the way. And then the lawless one will be revealed, whom the Lord Jesus will kill with the breath of his mouth and bring to nothing by the appearance of his coming. The coming of the lawless one is by the activity of Satan with all power and false signs and wonders, and with all wicked deception for those who are

[a] 2 Thessalonians 2:12

86

perishing, because they refused to love the truth and so be saved. Therefore God sends them a strong delusion, so that they may believe what is false, in order that all may be condemned who did not believe the truth but had pleasure in unrighteousness.[a]

The Last Days delusion will be so powerful that even some who profess to be Christians but do not possess saving faith will fall away and join the man of lawlessness. Some churches, pulpits, and even entire denominations will get caught up in the frenzy of worshiping a counterfeit Christ who will be a political leader.

Globalism is Godless

The only hope for everyone and everything is the Second Coming of Jesus Christ at the final moment in history, when the anti-Christ man of lawlessness rises up to rule the two kingdoms – both Church and state. How incredible is this scene! The most powerful person ruled by Satan in the history of the earth is brought to nothing by one single breath from the mouth of our God and Savior, the Lord Jesus Christ!

The storyline of the Bible is set against a backdrop of spiritual warfare. Satan and his demons were cast out of God's Kingdom for trying a coup attempt to remove and replace Jesus Christ as King.[b] Satan then tempted our first parents, Adam and Eve, to come under his dominion instead of God's. When they did, humanity lost its dominion, and Satan became the "god of this world."[c] Showing himself as spiritual king over the nations, in tempting Jesus, Matthew 4:8-9 says,

[a] 2 Thessalonians 2:3-12 [b] Revelation 12:7-9 [c] 2 Corinthians 4:4

"Again, the devil took him to a very high mountain and showed him all the kingdoms of the world and their glory. And he said to him, 'All these I will give you, if you will fall down and worship me.'" Over and over, we see Satan at work behind the scenes in nations throughout the Bible. His plan is to create a global government over which he can rule as the counterfeit of the King of Kings once and for all.

For example, in Jesus' day, the Roman Empire was the largest and most powerful on earth, an attempt at globalism as an "imperial cult." Today, we treat politicians like saviors and campaigns with all the enthusiasm of a religious crusade, which is much like the days when Jesus walked around the Roman Empire.

> Understanding the nature of early Christianity and the New Testament texts depends on understanding the practice of religion in the Roman Empire. Several features distinguish religion in the Graeco-Roman period from religion in Western cultures:
> 1. Religion permeated all aspects of culture, in both public and private life.
> 2. Roman policy included a commitment to polytheism; the acceptance and integration of additional gods was part of that commitment.
> 3. Certain Roman cultural values and social institutions were held to be religious in nature so that ideals such as masculinity, honor, and the patronage system were essential features of the practice of Roman religion...In the Graeco-Roman world, religion permeated all aspects of culture; there was no separation between the secular and the sacred...[45]

Lastly, like most devout Jewish believers in His day, Jesus did not syncretize His faith with the imperial cult. Instead, He paid His taxes and honored authority, but He did not compromise His integrity by engaging in all the paganism that surrounded the worship of the emperor. By declaring Himself Lord, Jesus was seen as a threat to the imperial cult that worshiped Caesar as lord, which is why the Roman government ultimately put Him to death. We know from the Bible that Satan and other demonic forces were at work behind the scenes in the Roman government, and the same forces were at work in the political leadership of Babylon in the days of Daniel, which we will study next.

CHAPTER 9
What is the Demonic Political Spirit of Babylon?

Revelation 14:8 – Another angel, a second, followed, saying, "Fallen, fallen is Babylon the great, she who made all nations drink the wine of the passion of her sexual immorality."

When the same evils happen in different nations and generations, how can those similarities be explained since the political leaders are different? Although people come and go, the demons working through them remain the same. Although we have new days, we are dealing with old demons.

As we have learned, the first attempt at globalism was in ancient Babel. Babylon is the same place where the people came from 1,500 years later to invade Jerusalem and lay siege to God's city. They killed and enslaved God's people, including Daniel, taking them captive as prisoners of war. In Babylon, King Nebuchadnezzar built a large statue like the Tower of Babel so that everyone could worship him as a counterfeit god.[a] The point is this: we keep seeing the same things happen from one generation to the next. Why? Because people change, but demons don't. Nations change, but demons don't. Demons will work

[a] Daniel 3:1-7

through one person or one government, and when that person or government transitions, the new person or government is overtaken by the same demon. Genesis and Daniel are not just about what happened – they're about what always happens. Ultimately, the same spirits at work in their day are at work in our own day.

What is the Spirit of Babylon?

For the original readers of Daniel, the nations and kings would be as familiar to us as the high-profile nations and political leaders on the world stage that dominate our nightly news. As a bit of a history lesson to set the stage for the book of Daniel, Babylon and the Babylonians are also called Chaldea and the Chaldeans throughout the Bible. Babylon is an ancient nation, but it's important to note that behind Babylon was the demonic spirit of Babylon. In fact, Nebuchadnezzar saw himself as the king over the globe, sending out decrees, saying in Daniel 4:1, "...to all peoples, nations, and languages, that dwell in all the earth..." God creates a Kingdom that is called His bride. Satan counterfeits with a kingdom that is called Babylon, the "mother of prostitutes."ᵃ The demonic spirit of Babylon is at work in every nation and generation. For this reason, the last book of the Bible, Revelation, is closely connected to Daniel, as they both have prophecies about the end of human history and the beginning of eternity with the Second Coming of Jesus Christ. Long after the nation of Babylon had ceased to exist, Revelation reveals that the demonic spirit of Babylon remains at work in the world.

•Revelation 14:8: Another angel, a second,

ᵃ Revelation 17:5

followed, saying, "Fallen, fallen is Babylon the great, she who made all nations drink the wine of the passion of her sexual immorality."

- Revelation 16:19: The great city was split into three parts, and the cities of the nations fell, and God remembered Babylon the great, to make her drain the cup of the wine of the fury of his wrath.
- Revelation 17:5: ...on her forehead was written a name of mystery: "Babylon the great, mother of prostitutes and of earth's abominations."
- Revelation 18:1-2: ...I saw another angel coming down from heaven, having great authority, and the earth was made bright with his glory. And he called out with a mighty voice, "Fallen, fallen is Babylon the great! She has become a dwelling place for demons, a haunt for every unclean spirit, a haunt for every unclean bird, a haunt for every unclean and detestable beast."
- Revelation 18:10: They will stand far off, in fear of her torment, and say, "Alas! Alas! You great city, you mighty city, Babylon! For in a single hour your judgment has come."
- Revelation 18:21: Then a mighty angel took up a stone like a great millstone and threw it into the sea, saying, "So will Babylon the great city be thrown down with violence, and will be found no more..."

The demonic spirit of Babylon was in Sodom and Gomorrah and Nazi Germany, is in North Korea and Iran, runs drug cartels and human trafficking, is writing curriculum for students, is architecting political platforms and cultural narratives in everything from movies to television shows, and enjoys surfing the internet and causing social media trends. No one, no thing, and no place is immune from the demonic influence of the spirit of Babylon.

Babylon was corrupt to the core. It was the largest and most powerful nation on earth in its day, a superpower with a deadly military, a strong economy, and demonic power. Everything from politics to entertainment, gender, sexuality, and education was ungodly, unhealthy, and unbiblical. Daniel was trapped in a world that he could not control and was pressured to think and act like a

Babylonian, which would have made his life easier at the cost of losing his relationship with God. Simply stated, Daniel was forced to decide between living as a believer or a Babylonian. He was in a pressing vice between the two kingdoms. In the opening chapter of Daniel, he and three other young men (likely teenagers) were stripped of their birth names and instead had the government legally change their names. Each name change is an attempt to forcibly convert them from devotion to the true God to devotion to the demonic spirits worshiped as gods.

In naming the young men, we see that the spirit of Babylon that exists in every nation and culture is always seeking to change our identity and loyalty from the true God to the counterfeit demonic gods. Throughout the book of Daniel, the young men are called by their new names by the Babylonians, but curiously, they never refer to themselves by those new demonic names. The point is that our identity must be set by our God, no matter what the government says. Today, for example, there is great pressure on younger generations to deny their God-given identity as being created male and female and adopt a worldly and pagan identity instead.

Worldly cultures can change your name, but only God can change your nature. It doesn't matter what others put on you; it only matters that God's Spirit is in you. In many ways, Daniel is a case study in the principles of living as a missionary in this world with godless government, as found in 1 Peter 2:11-12 (NLT): "Dear friends, I warn you as 'temporary residents and foreigners' to keep away from worldly desires that wage war against your very souls. Be careful to live properly among your unbelieving neighbors. Then even if they accuse you of doing wrong, they will see your honorable behavior, and they will give honor to God when he judges the world."

7 Signs of the Spirit of Babylon

Babylon, and the demonic spirit of Babylon, is marked by seven actions that we see in Daniel and continuing today with such things as wokeism (which is the new term for cultural Marxism) and the ensuing deconstruction of everything from sex to gender, marriage, family, and even God.

1. *Cross Borders*: In the days of Daniel, the Babylonians crossed the border into Israel, invading the nation to ultimately overtake it. 2 Kings 25:8-10 says,

> In the fifth month, on the seventh day of the month—that was the nineteenth year of King Nebuchadnezzar, king of Babylon— Nebuzaradan, the captain of the bodyguard, a servant of the king of Babylon, came to Jerusalem. And he burned the house of the Lord and the king's house and all the houses of Jerusalem; every great house he burned down. And all the army of the Chaldeans, who were with the captain of the guard, broke down the walls around Jerusalem.

Because the demonic spirit of Babylon is a spirit of globalism, it continuously seeks to remove borders and walls that divide nations. The walls torn down by King Nebuchadnezzar, for example, lay in ruins until they were rebuilt by Nehemiah. Today, the demonic spirit of Babylon has, in effect, torn down the "walls" or southern border in America, allowing more than 10 million illegal aliens to enter the nation during the current administration, many from known terrorist nations committed to the destruction of the nation.

2. *Close Churches*: In the days of Daniel, the spirit of Babylon tore down the worship altars, closed the churches, and stopped the worship of God in one nation. During the COVID "pandemic," the demonic spirit of Babylon went global, shutting down the Church in every nation for Easter – something that had never happened in world history. In many nations, including my own, the abortion clinics were open on Easter while the churches were closed. Consider that fact for a moment: churches called to preach the gospel of eternal life were closed because it was said to help save human lives, and clinics were open so that abortion could remain the leading cause of death. The entire scenario is demonic.

3. *Control Schools*: In the days of Daniel, the Bible reports that the demonic spirit of Babylon working through the government closed the Bible-based schools of the prophets so that only government schools remained open to indoctrinate future generations. Today, the death grip that the government has on education is made possible by the demonic spirit of Babylon, which wants children killed in the womb, and if they're not killed, they can be controlled and indoctrinated.

4. *Cancel Prophets*: In the days of Daniel, those believers with a prophetic function of calling the nation to repentance lost their platforms, were canceled, and eventually were killed. Today, cancel culture focuses almost entirely on

conservatives, which is, in fact, the ongoing anti-ministry of the demonic spirit of Babylon.

5. *Counterfeit Prophets*: In the days of Daniel, numerous false prophets worked by demonic power to advise the king. They are referred to as magicians, enchanters, sorcerers, Chaldeans, and the wise men of Babylon.ᵃ A false prophet is someone who claims to speak for God or know the future, which is untrue. Today, the media and social media are filled with counterfeit false prophets, causing people to live under the demonic spirit of fear in everything from the economy to politics and pandemics and predicting things that never happen.

6. *Create Perversion*: Ancient Babylon was known for its sexual violence and perversion. "In Babylonian law, only a wife could be guilty of adultery...If a married person had sex with an unmarried person, only the married person was considered guilty...The testimony of a woman who had been raped was not considered evidence..."[46] God rebuked Babylon for their sexual perversion in Isaiah 47 saying,

> Your nakedness shall be uncovered, and your disgrace shall be seen. I will take vengeance, and I will spare no one...for you shall no more be called the mistress of kingdoms... Now therefore hear this, you lover of pleasures...These two things shall come to you in a moment, in one day; the loss of children and widowhood shall come upon you in full measure, in spite of your many sorceries and the great power of your

ᵃ Daniel 2, 4, 5

enchantments.

In Daniel 5:2, we read that men and women were together at a lavish state party. This was uncommon in the ancient world, as Babylon was one of the only nations where the women did not dine at such events separate from the men and "at Babylon they were not noted for their modesty on such occasions."[47]
In Revelation, the demonic sexual spirit of Babylon is referred to as responsible for "all nations drink[ing] the wine of...passion" (14:8), as well as being the "mother of prostitutes" (17:5) and a "dwelling place for demons" (18:2). Today, the spirit of Babylon is seducing nations into perversion that leads to destruction in everything from transgenderism, Pride month, the porn industry, adult entertainment, sex trafficking, the sexualization of minors, the push to lower the age of sexual consent, and criticism of heterosexual monogamous marriage as outdated and restrictive.

7. *Castrate Youth*: One often overlooked aspect of Daniel's 70-plus years in Babylon is that his genitalia were most likely mutilated by castration as a healthy young man. This was prophesied in Isaiah 39:5-7:

> Hear the word of the Lord of hosts: Behold, the days are coming, when all that is in your house, and that which your fathers have stored up till this day, shall be carried to Babylon. Nothing shall be left, says the Lord. And some of your own sons, who will come from you, whom you will father, shall be taken away, and they shall be eunuchs in the

palace of the king of Babylon.

In Daniel 1, he is overseen by a government "eunuch" and trained to serve in the palace. It was common in the ancient world for men working for the king in the palace to be castrated so that they did not sexually pursue the king's harem who was also living in the palace. For example, we also read about Queen Jezebel's "eunuchs" in the days of the prophet Elijah.[a] The fact that Daniel never marries or has any romantic relationships also points to the likelihood that the demonic spirit of Babylon had him castrated. Today, the spirit of Babylon is doing the same evil – causing the genital mutilation and gender confusion of an entire generation of healthy young people.

There comes a point with a godless government that godly people start wondering if they should push back, something we will study next.

THE DEMOCRATIC MARATHON

[a] 2 Kings 9:32

CHAPTER 10
What is Civil Disobedience?

Proverbs 29:2 – When the righteous increase, the people rejoice, but when the wicked rule, the people groan.

In the days of the American Civil Rights movement, there was a hotly debated issue within the African American community between violent versus non-violent civil disobedience. Both sides agreed that the government had been unjust in its' treatment of black people, from slavery to Jim Crow laws enforcing racial segregation, with the legal system wrongly stacked for white people and against black people. Two leaders emerged with divergent responses. Malcolm X taught violent civil disobedience when necessary, whereas Martin Luther King, Jr. espoused non-violent means of pressuring the government for legal changes, often working with black churches. In fact, Martin Luther King, Jr. won the Nobel Peace Prize in 1955. In addition, Rosa Parks loved Jesus, and she was driven by biblical convictions. When told to move to the back of her bus, Rosa refused because she believed every person is made equally in the image of God. This refusal was an act of civil disobedience. To this day, these are the two primary versions of civil disobedience: violent and non-violent.

When there is a conflict between God and government, what do you do? How can you live as both a good resident of your nation and a faithful citizen of God's Kingdom? Civil disobedience is defined as a public, non-violent, and conscientious act contrary to the law, usually done with the intent of bringing about a change in the policies or laws of the government. Civil disobedience happens in two ways.

1. The government commands you to do something God forbids.
2. The government forbids you to do something God commands.

When considering civil disobedience, we must be careful not to base our decisions on misinformation or disinformation. So many wild, inappropriate, and erroneous things are shared on the internet, and this includes both left- and right-wing conspiracy theories. We must learn to discern what is true and false, and if we do respond, we must respond in a way that rightly represents our faith.

American culture is trending against faith, freedom, and family. As Christians, we need to avail ourselves of legal, right, and honorable ways of affecting culture change.

Just and Unjust States

Before examining biblical examples of godly civil disobedience, it is important to note that today, the issue of civil disobedience against an unjust government is considered on the back of two world wars and the attempt at demonic globalism by Adolf Hitler.

In the ethical debate after World War Two

KEEP AWAY FROM IT!

RUM PUNCH

— THE DEMOCRATIC SITUATION —

about attitudes toward totalitarian states, a new trend began to emerge. Now it is a much more widespread and accepted standard of ethics that the people, Christians included, have the right and even the duty to resist an unjust, demonic state. For centuries it had been hammered in, especially in the Roman Catholic and Lutheran churches, that it is Christian to obey every governing authority, without regard to possibly unethical decisions and claims. The obligation to submit to even a bad, evil and unjust state was considered to be part of God's hidden governance and upbringing of his people. Disobedience and resistance could lead to anarchy, which was contrary to God's will—

according to the common understanding. This traditional attitude was adjusted through the terrible experiences of the Third Reich. The attempt to kill Hitler on 20 July 1944 has to a great extent been justified since the war in theological thinking...The change in this respect can be illustrated by an example from the struggle of the Church of Norway against Nazism during the German occupation of 1940-45.[48]

Following the World Wars, Christian scholars spent considerable time studying and debating what qualifies as an unjust state.

The bishop of Oslo, Eivind Berggrav, made a sharp distinction between a just and an unjust state—a distinction which was appropriate at that time. The just state, the bishop reasoned, is based on a theological interpretation of natural law. The law, a constituent part of the state, is considered holy...[and] corresponds to God's will for creation (lex creationis). His criteria for a just state seemed to be the following:
(1) The just state acts in accordance with law and justice, which are anchored in God.
(2) The just state is limited to temporal matters; it is not allowed to influence questions of faith and conscience.
(3) The just state has to keep brutal and crude power under control by upholding the law and administering justice.
(4) The just state is able to distinguish between good and evil deeds, and it does not hinder the former.[49]

Godly Civil Disobedience

Scripture offers many stories of godly civil disobedience. Let's begin with examples of things the government commands you to do that God forbids. In Exodus, Pharaoh feared the people of Israel were growing so numerous that his slaves would form an insurrection against his government. Pharaoh decided to murder all Hebrew males; this was government-sponsored infanticide. The Hebrew midwives refused to take innocent human lives and practiced civil disobedience by allowing the males to live, including Moses, who would eventually deliver God's people out of slavery. The Bible honors these Hebrew midwives by telling us their names: Shiphrah ("beautiful") and Puah ("fragrant blossom").

Another example of civil disobedience in the Old Testament is Joseph. He served as a slave (having no legal rights) to the government leader, Potiphar, and his wife. Potiphar's wife "cast her eyes on Joseph and said, 'Lie with me.'"[a] She commanded him to commit adultery. Joseph refused, saying, "How can I do this great wickedness and sin against God?"[b] This refusal was an act of civil disobedience because Joseph didn't have the right to say no to any Egyptian official for any reason. Potiphar's wife responded by falsely accusing him of rape, and her enraged husband had Joseph thrown into prison.

Centuries later, a female prostitute named Rahab lived in Jericho, where government officials had heard rumors that there were Israelite spies in the area and that the people of Israel were coming to overtake their city. Anyone who knew anything about these spies was ordered to share that

[a] Genesis 39:7 [b] Genesis 39:9

information with the government. Rahab hid the spies on her roof under bundles of flax, lied about their whereabouts, and helped them escape. Lying is almost always a sin, but when you are preserving human life, it is an act of civil disobedience and worship. When the Israelites later came and destroyed the city, Rahab and her family were saved. She converted to faith in the one true God and eventually became the mother of Boaz, who was the husband of Ruth, and an ancestor of Jesus Christ. Rahab is listed among the greatest heroes of the Christian faith in Hebrews 11.

The opening words of the 10 Commandments tell us there is one God, and we are to worship Him alone. Shadrach, Meshach, and Abednego – Daniel's three Hebrew friends taken to Babylon in

the Exile – held fast to this command in the face of tremendous opposition. King Nebuchadnezzar made a 300-foot-tall statue of himself and demanded everyone bow down and worship him as head of the two kingdoms. They refused, knowing the consequence of this civil disobedience could be death by burning in a fiery furnace.

Jesus' earthly parents, Mary and Joseph, practiced civil disobedience. When Jesus was born, word got to Herod, the local political leader, that the King of Kings and Lord of Lords was born. Herod refused to have his authority threatened, so he tried to have Jesus murdered. When that didn't work, Herod put a death sentence on a whole generation of firstborn Hebrew boys. Jesus' parents left Israel and fled to Egypt. Rather than submitting to the government and the murder of their Son, they lived in another nation until the political regime changed.

In addition, Jesus Himself practiced civil disobedience. In that day, the highest pledge of loyalty was to the state: "Caesar is lord." But Jesus couldn't say that because it wasn't true, and His followers wouldn't say it either. They proclaimed, "Jesus Christ is Lord," and for that, they were harassed, arrested, and martyred.

Scripture also offers examples of civil disobedience when the government forbids believers to do something God commands.

In the days of Elijah, Obadiah disobeyed the command of King Ahab and his demonic wife Jezebel and hid God's servants so they would not be arrested and put to death.

In the days of Daniel, the Babylonian government forbade praying to the one true God for 30 days. Despite this command, Daniel continued to pray three times a day. He broke government law to obey God's law, and as a result, he was thrown into a den of lions. God was faithful to Daniel; He shut the lions' mouths and allowed no harm to come to His servant. When he discovered Daniel was still alive, King Darius praised God and made a decree that everyone in the kingdom should "tremble and fear before the God of Daniel."[a]

Jesus' apostles were commanded to stop preaching in the name of Jesus, and the apostles were arrested and beaten for doing so. Still, the apostles responded, "...we cannot but speak of what we have seen and heard."[b]

The apostle Paul spent years of his life in prison for preaching the gospel. Paul even wrote many of his letters in the Bible behind bars. He started riots by simply preaching the gospel. Every time there is a revival in the Spirit, there is a riot in the demonic. When Paul came to a village or town, many people put their faith in Jesus Christ, but those who did not would often start a riot. For every action, there was a reaction, and for every convert, there was a critic. We don't know exactly how Paul died, but most scholars believe he was beheaded by the godless government.

For those of us who love Jesus, being a faithful, Bible-believing, sin-repenting citizen of God's Kingdom and resident of our nation is going to bring varying degrees of difficulty into our lives. By being good citizens, Christians can earn trusted positions within government from which they can do good. The Bible provides many examples – Joseph ruling in Egypt, Nehemiah ruling in Persia, and Daniel ruling in Babylon. By being good citizens, Christians can also keep a low profile, so they have liberty to live and worship freely with minimal intrusion.

There are times, however, when God and

[a] Daniel 6:26 [b] Acts 4:20

the government have different demands, and a person is forced to consider if they should flee, work through the system for more just laws or new political leaders, or simply disobey the government in obedience to God.

- Titus 3:1-2: Remind them to be submissive to rulers and authorities, to be obedient, to be ready for every good work, to speak evil of no one, to avoid quarreling, to be gentle, and to show perfect courtesy toward all people.
- 1 Peter 2:13-17: Be subject for the Lord's sake to every human institution, whether it be to the emperor as supreme, or to governors as sent by him to punish those who do evil and to praise those who do good. For this is the will of God, that by doing good you should

put to silence the ignorance of foolish people.
Live as people who are free, not using
your freedom as a cover-up for evil, but living
as servants of God. Honor everyone. Love the
brotherhood. Fear God. Honor the emperor.

To faithfully understand the Bible, we must
examine not just what the authors said but also
what they did. These statements from Paul and
Peter, at face value, seem to state that there should
never be civil disobedience against the government.
However, we know that both men were jailed by the
government for breaking godless laws. In the days
of the New Testament, there were four primary
ways that religious people responded to their
godless government, which we will examine in the
next four chapters.

CHAPTER 11
Should Christians Live Off the Grid and Ignore Politics Like the Ancient Essenes?

Jeremiah 48:6 – Flee! Save yourselves! You will be like a juniper in the desert!

In Jesus' day, there were four basic models of interaction with the world that He could have adopted, but He adopted none of them. Some of these groups are referred to in the Bible as "parties," and others would technically be called "sects." These are a lot like political parties in our day – groups of people with leaders and convictions that seek to reduce the influence of other parties on government, Church, and culture while converting people to their party to increase their power and influence. For example, the Bible mentions the "high priest" and "the party of the Sadducees" or "all who were with him."[a] We also read about "the party of the Pharisees" and those "who belonged to the party."[b] Oddly, the Pharisee party is also called the "circumcision party," which seems like the worst possible party you could attend, no matter how good the snacks and band are.[c]

[a] Acts 5:17 [b] Acts 15:5 [c] Acts 11:2; Galatians 2:12; Titus 1:10

4 FAITH FACTIONS

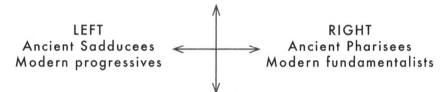

FIGHT
Ancient Zealots
Modern civil disobedience

LEFT
Ancient Sadducees
Modern progressives

RIGHT
Ancient Pharisees
Modern fundamentalists

FLEE
Ancient Essenes
Modern homesteaders

The Zealots chose to march forward and sought to overthrow the government by force if necessary.

The Essenes sought to retreat backward, largely exiting politics and culture, to live quiet private lives.

The Pharisees veered to the right, becoming a legalistic religious subculture marked by infighting.

The Sadducees veered to the left, becoming cultural progressives who compromised their faith to hold positions of political and cultural influence.

Believers Off the Grid

The Essenes were basically off-grid ancient Hebrew preppers who probably spoke in tongues. They lost hope that the greater culture could be redeemed, and rather than fighting against it, they retreated from it. Like the Pharisees, they believed in the total corruption of the world, including politics, and rather than trying to carve out a subculture, they chose to live in smaller private rural communities with like-minded believers.

The Essenes would have resonated with the story of Noah. In his day, everyone and everything was so evil that it could not be redeemed, so it was destroyed by a flood. Noah built an ark that saved his family, and although no one else wanted to be saved, at least Noah had a safe place for the people he loved most to survive. The story of Lot would also be a good comparison. Lot's family was living in Sodom and Gomorrah and fled to the hills before God destroyed everyone and everything. This kind of sentiment was at the heart of the Essene experiment: the fallen world is beyond hope, so, before society collapses, the best thing to do is get the people you love to a safe place far away from the implosion.

The Essenes perceived themselves as a remnant of true believers being kept by God. In this way, they resonated with the Old Testament story of Elijah, who lives a bit like an Essene – a mountain man and prophet with supernatural power who lived a very private life in the woods and only came into town to function as a prophet and rebuke the godless King Ahab and Queen Jezebel, who had led the nation into apostasy. In 1 Kings 18, along with Elijah, there was a community of 100 prophets who were kept hidden in caves, grouped into 50 each, and fed by Obadiah, a man of God working for the demonic government but secretly protecting God's servants.

Very little is known about the Essenes because they were remote and private. The Dead Sea Scrolls are often associated with this rather secret society, and only a few historians have any reports to share because outsiders were not welcome, and insiders did not divulge details of their separated lives. One of the vows taken to become an Essene was a lifelong commitment to not divulging any details about the religious community.

Historians are unsure what the name Essene even means. Furthermore, it was very difficult for someone to join an Essene community.

> Those who wanted to join the sect were not
> immediately received into the group but were
> given prescribed clothing and equipment and
> proper food to eat in separate quarters. Only
> after two...or three...years of probation, if the
> candidate was observed to be "worthy"...he
> was admitted to the inner circle.[50]

The Essenes' entire community functioned much like a close-knit small church in a rural area far away from other people and provisions. They would not take oaths, they shared possessions and ate meals together, and their strength was in a community that was perhaps a bit like the Amish.

They took good care of each other. They had very strict rules governing their daily activities, so they became very legalistic like the Pharisees. The big idea is this: the more closed your group, the more legalistic it becomes, and here's why: unbelievers and new believers ask a lot of questions that keep you rethinking what you believe and why you believe it. Without these people, religious tradition begins to multiply until legalisms are simply assumed to be the way of holiness. For example, they had weird, strict regulations about when and where you could go to the bathroom, and you were supposed to hold it for the entire Sabbath so as not to defile that holy day.

In addition, they wanted to identify themselves as pure, so they'd only wear white. They refused to participate in Temple sacrifices. They were very concerned about personal holiness. They rejected sexual intercourse for pleasure, saying it was only for procreation. These would be the hyper-spiritual folks in our day who spend all their time in prayer meetings, praying loudly in tongues, enjoying all-night worship events, seeking signs and wonders, and speculating about the end of the world while keeping strict personal holiness standards and judging other believers who do not hold those same legalisms.

Around 175 B.C., the Maccabean Revolt caused the Essenes to become very popular. Hellenism sought to remove Jewish belief and replace it with Greek philosophy and culture. This syncretism replaced the worship of Yahweh with Zeus and banned all Jewish festivals and practices. Jews had to flee the city and go underground to practice their faith, much like the underground persecuted Church in our day. Generally, the Essenes would have a lot in common politically with the Pharisees, except they were pacifists. They didn't want to fight; they didn't want to take up arms. In this way, the Essenes were the counterbalance to the Zealots, who were the warriors.

Essene theology was very much compelled by spiritual warfare and biblical themes such as darkness versus light and good versus evil. They were very interested in prophecy, events surrounding the End Times, the Holy Spirit, and spiritual power, which makes them much like Pentecostals and Charismatics in our day. However, they also believed in God's providence, which agreed with the Pharisees and disagreed with the Sadducees.

They were fascinated with angels and demons, including personal angels. They believed in Heaven and Hell and the resurrection of the dead, like the Pharisees and unlike the Sadducees. Unlike the Sadducees, who ignored parts of the Bible that reduced their approval as cultural elites from the secular culture, and unlike the Pharisees, who added a lot of legalism and tradition to God's Word, the Essenes were fully committed to the Scriptures as their highest authority.

However, the Essenes did leave opportunities for prophetic words. Josephus, the ancient historian, reports that their Essene prophet, Menahem, prophesied that Herod would be king. That prophecy came to pass, and the Essenes were known for this kind of supernatural revelation about political issues. However, because they were isolated and fearful, the Essenes were also vulnerable to wild conspiracy theories, much like those who live on the fringes of the internet today, trying to pull together strands of political and cultural happenings with off-the-wall interpretations of Bible passages.

Are Essenes in the Bible?

Do we find any Essenes in the Bible? At the very least, no one is clearly stated to be an Essene. There is a highly debated belief that maybe John the Baptizer was at least somehow related to the Essenes. After all, he lived in the woods and only came into town as a prophet to rebuke the king, which caused the government to behead him. He was not with the Pharisees or the Sadducees. He was not trained within the formal religious institutions of that day or part of an established religious party. God just anoints him in the Spirit, and he shows up out of the woods looking a little crazy, proclaiming repentance. He looks and acts a lot like Elijah, and he comes with the same Holy Spirit anointing. There is a television show called "Alone" where outdoor survivalists are dropped into remote areas utterly alone with only a few items. They must build shelter, obtain water, hunt food, and manage a fire to remain alive. The person who can endure this rugged lifestyle the longest without tapping out emotionally or physically each season is declared the winner. Elijah or John the Baptizer would have won this show because both were rugged mountain men and looked every bit the part.[a]

Today, the equivalent of the Essene would include those believers who are certain that the end of the world is near and demonic influence has so overtaken politics and culture that it is unredeemable. They'd say the best thing to do is move off-grid onto a large piece of land in the middle of nowhere, surround yourself with like-minded believers, keep to yourself, avoid and ignore the outside world, take care of one

[a] 2 Kings 1:8; Matthew 3:4

117

another, and spend your days being spiritual and practicing for Heaven by praying, speaking in tongues, worshiping, and prophesying. These groups distrust outside sources, and today they would reject the mainstream media, for example, as thoroughly corrupt, which causes them to disbelieve most anything they hear from outside of their list of approved information sources. Furthermore, believers today who are preparing for the end of the world with such things as bunkers and food rations hold a lot in common with the ancient Essenes.

Christians Packing Up and Leaving Liberal Cities

Today, there is also a modified version of the Essenes. In our age of great mobility, conservative Christians are leaving liberal cities in large numbers to either live in more rural small towns or more conservative large cities. Often, their driving motivation is the well-being of future generations of children and grandchildren.

If they still live within the mandates of Scripture, guard against the demonic spirit of fear, and feel compelled by their conscience to exit society and live a quiet, private life for God, the Essene option is a viable one for some Christians. In the Old Testament, the nation of Israel functioned as a closed community surrounded by pagan nations. Throughout the history of Christianity, there have also been similar monastic communities in every generation – many fleeing completely corrupt cultures and attempting to live out their faith in private with fellow believers.

There are some Scriptures that seem to point toward an Essene lifestyle:
•John 15:19 (NLT): The world would love you

as one of its own if you belonged to it, but you are no longer part of the world. I chose you to come out of the world, so it hates you.

- Romans 12:2: Do not be conformed to this world...
- 2 Corinthians 6:17 (HCSB): Therefore, come out from among them and be separate, says the Lord...
- 1 Thessalonians 4:11-12: ...aspire to live quietly, and to mind your own affairs, and to work with your hands, as we instructed you, so that you may walk properly before outsiders and be dependent on no one.
- 2 Thessalonians 3:12: Now such persons we command and encourage in the Lord Jesus Christ to do their work quietly and to earn their own living.
- 1 Timothy 2:1-2: First of all, then, I urge that supplications, prayers, intercessions, and thanksgivings be made for all people, for kings and all who are in high positions, that we may lead a peaceful and quiet life, godly and dignified in every way.
- 1 John 2:16-17: For all that is in the world—the desires of the flesh and the desires of the eyes and pride of life—is not from the Father but is from the world. And the world is passing away along with its desires, but whoever does the will of God abides forever.
- James 4:4: You adulterous people! Do you not know that friendship with the world is enmity with God? Therefore whoever wishes to be a friend of the world makes himself an enemy of God.

Other Scriptures seem to indicate the Essene path for God's people to avoid impending danger, especially from demonic governments. For example,

Jacob[a], David[b], Rehoboam[c], Amos[d], and Zechariah[e] are all told to "flee." Moses[f] and Jesus Christ[g] also both fled to private places to avoid being killed by the government.

However, if all believers take the Essene path, the problem is that there is no one left to represent God in the culture or reach the lost with the gospel. Jesus says in Matthew 5:13–16 that we are the salt and light of the world. If the world is dark, some Christians need to stay in it to bring the light of God. The world is like meat, rotting away. Believers are like salt that keeps meat from deteriorating as quickly. The presence of God's people in a nation helps preserve its' life and keep things from rotting as quickly. If most or all of God's people leave a society, it becomes fully dark and quickly rotten. This is why Jesus prayed in John 17:15, "I do not ask that you take them out of the world, but that you keep them from the evil one." Whether or not believers should ever attack the government is a question we will answer next.

[a] Genesis 27:43 [b] 2 Samuel 15:14 [c] 1 Kings 12:18 [d] Amos 7:12
[e] Zechariah 2:5-7 [f] Exodus 2 [g] Matthew 2

CHAPTER 12
Should Christians Seek to Overthrow the Government Like the Ancient Zealots?

Matthew 10:34 – "Do not think that I [Jesus] have come to bring peace to the earth. I have not come to bring peace, but a sword."

Today, perhaps the most rigidly controlled nation on earth is North Korea. Ruled with an iron fist and totalitarian power, the North Korean government does not allow any ideology that competes with the Juche belief system. It controls every aspect of culture, requires the ruler to be worshiped as God, and has outlawed Christianity to the point that most of its' citizens have never even heard the name of Jesus Christ.

Juche theory is a type of Marxism ideology, but it is built upon the deification and mystification of Kim Il-sung (1912-1994). Its religious or pseudo-religious characteristics distinguish Juche ideology from all other forms of Marxism...Juche ideology characterizes Kim as the "eternal head of state," a Messianic liberator of humankind, and describes North Korea as a chosen nation, and North Koreans as a chosen people who have a mission to liberate the world. While fear and terror are used to externally dominate the masses in a totalitarian state, Juche Ideology is a tool for the internal domination of their minds (known as hegemony).[51]

Juche is a counterfeit of the Kingdom of God that makes Kim Il-sung a counterfeit Jesus by teaching that, after he died, he continued to rule eternally as a spiritual god. His birthplace and other noteworthy places in his life are considered holy places that people make religious pilgrimages to. His photo hangs in every home, and every citizen is forced to begin each day by reciting his words. Legally, every paragraph of the preface of the constitution venerates him, and worship of this man is the center of the entire legal system. Anyone who disagrees with this man is considered a traitor and can be sentenced to death. Furthermore,

> In the constitution of North Korea written in 1998, Kim Il-sung was described as the "eternal head of state." According to the materialist philosophy of Marxism, there is no "eternal" entity such as God or beings that exist in the realm of a spiritual world. Accordingly, the Eternal Tower was built as a material symbol of the eternal presence of Kim. Kim was described as a "political parent" who was said to be present with people as long as they held this ideology. Furthermore, as Gregorian calendars date from the birth of Jesus, North Korea adopted its own calendar dating from the birth of Kim Il-sung.[52]

For Christians seeking to live a faithful life to Jesus Christ in North Korea today, their only option seems to be violent civil disobedience like the ancient Jewish Zealots. The one thing that the ancient Pharisees, Sadducees, Essenes, and Zealots held in common was a dislike and distrust of the Roman government, even though their proposed responses were very different. The Pharisees' goal was to work around Roman government and culture by separating from it into a subculture. The Sadducees' goal was to completely embrace, adopt, and live in it as respected by and received in pagan society. The Essenes' goal was to abandon Roman government and culture, fleeing to rural areas to create a separate culture. The Zealots' goal was to destroy, overtake, and replace the Roman government altogether and usher in wholesale cultural change.

The Essenes were the pacifists who largely avoided conflict and culture, and the Zealots were their counterbalance as they were an armed militia. The Zealots' goal was simple: live prepared for a bloody revolution.

Onward Christian Soldier

The Zealots were basically a religious party that was like a militia. They were a resistance party, very devoted to politics, and zealous, as their name suggests. Zeal, as a rule, is not bad. Even a quick search of the Bible reveals that God speaks favorably of zeal, so long as the cause and means are just. The Zealots' problem was that their zeal for God caused them to do things that were ungodly. In every age, there is a temptation to wrongly believe that the ends justify the means. Today, the equivalent of the Zealots would be those who talk a lot about Jesus but plan for jihad.

Both ancient and modern Zealots function as a political military resistance movement. The Zealots in the ancient world were driven by their "prophets," who said if there was a coordinated attack on the Roman government in the name of God, God would bless that insurrection, cause military victory, and send a political Messiah to rule and reign. Today, the spirit of the Zealots lives on with the fringe right-wing politics driven by Pentecostal "prophets" inciting the insurrection of government. They promise that a Messiah-like political ruler will be raised up by God or that Jesus Christ Himself will even return not just to rule a nation but all the nations. It was this driving vision that, for example, helped fuel the attempted overthrow of the American government on January 6, 2021, with an attack on the U.S. Capitol. The vision of the Zealots does not distinguish between the two kingdoms, and, for them, spiritual problems would be largely resolved by political means, starting with a holy war. The Zealots were constantly recruiting people to join their ranks.

In the Old Testament, we do see some zealous folks. The warriors of Phinehas opposed Baal worship.[a] Elijah slaughters the false demonic prophets of King Ahab and Queen Jezebel.[b] When Dinah is sexually assaulted by the Shechemites, her brothers respond by slaughtering everyone.[c] Those with the Zealots' frustration and desire for justice navigate toward those kinds of stories and say, "We need to get a sword; we need to go to war; we need to defend the honor of our God." Like the Essenes, but with different outcomes, what really contributed to the popularity of the Zealots was the Maccabean Revolt.

I grew up Catholic before I became a born-again Protestant Christian. The Catholic version of the canon of Scripture has a few extra books of the Bible, including 1-2 Maccabees. Personally, I think

[a] Numbers 25 [b] 1 Kings 18 [c] Genesis 34

these are good historical books that help give some details about events in the Bible (especially the book of Daniel) but should not be considered part of the inspired canon of Scripture.

In Daniel 11, we see five different political rulers and around 150 years of human history predicted in advance by God who knows everything that will happen in the future in perfect detail. A Bible teacher says, "Daniel 11 is one of the most remarkable chapters in the entire Bible," and another Bible commentator notes that "in the first 35 verses, there are at least 135 prophecies that have been literally fulfilled and can be corroborated by a study of the history of the period."[53]

A divine being, likely the angel Gabriel, tells Daniel what's going to happen in governments – a succession of four kings, and the last one is King Ahasuerus, also called Xerxes, who was a prominent figure elsewhere in Esther. This king married Esther, who became a believer in God.

Gabriel's message that he supports both Daniel (a spiritual leader) and Darius (a political leader) is a good reminder for us to pray for both our political and spiritual leaders. Even if they don't know the Lord, the Lord knows them, and the Lord can lead and guide them to make good decisions for us all.

Daniel 11 reports that Antiochus III (also known as Antiochus the Great) marched west towards the coastlands and was defeated multiple times. He was on his way home and died en route. This all brings us to the people of God in verse 21. His son, Antiochus Epiphanes, was a horrible ruler and would rise up and want to be the "god-man."

He was not in the bloodline of a royal family but instead overthrew his nephew and stole the throne. He had a godly high priest removed and a godless, demonic pagan priest put in his place. He would enter peace treaties with other rulers and, once they let their guard down, attack and slaughter them. He was a horrible, demonic man filled with the power of Satan. He ruled, reigned, and gained the allegiance of the people like a drug cartel; those who were closest to him would reap rewards for plundering others. He marched against the king of the south (the king of Egypt) and won because the king of Egypt was betrayed.

As Antiochus Epiphanes heads home, history records that this became one of the darkest moments in Jewish history. He passes by Israel and decides to attack them, since he had inherited a massive debt to the Roman Empire, because he knows their Temple is filled with gold. In three days, he and his army slaughtered 80,000 Jewish civilians (God's people). This was the family line through which Jesus would come. He wanted the worshipers of God killed. He wanted the Temple of God to shut down. It seemed like God's people were doomed. Jesus couldn't come if the Jewish people were destroyed, or the Temple was closed.

A Sword for the Lord

The set of historical books 1-2 Maccabees tells the story of what happened next. After Antiochus Epiphanes set up demon worship in the Temple of God, a simple, humble country priest, Mattathias, comes to the Temple to worship God. The soldiers tell him that he must offer a pagan sacrifice to a demon god, and he refuses. Another priest next to him says he will do it to gain favor with the evil king because of fear of man. The first priest steps forward and kills the priest who is willing to compromise his beliefs and sacrifice to a demon god in God's Temple. Mattathias makes himself leader of an insurrection, and the first five people to stand with him and fight alongside him are his five sons. They become the Maccabees militia. They recruit Jewish men to fight with them, tear down idols, kill idolators, and declare war. They demand that the church, or Temple of God, be kept pure for the worship of God because they were waiting for Jesus. Mattathias is ultimately killed but he had, just prior, appointed his son, Judah, to take his place. Antiochus fights back and sends 60,000 elite soldiers to destroy the people of God. Judah recruits 7,000 men from Old Covenant churches in the area, and they go up against these 60,000 trained soldiers. Before they went into battle, the Jewish soldiers got together, led by Mattathias' sons, and they prayed. And who won? The 7,000 believers!

The Maccabees won the fight against Antiochus Epiphanes and then God ultimately killed him. Earlier in Daniel, it was prophesied that he would be brought to death but not by human hands, and he literally died of a punctured bowel. There's no explanation for it, but his whole body literally got toxic, and he died. He was taken down by the finger of God. Then, God's people could open the Temple again now that they were finally home from Babylon and this evil ruler had been stopped. Once they got together, they were so excited that they created the holiday called Hanukkah or "Festival of Lights" because the light was on in the Temple. All

of this pointed to the coming of Jesus Christ as the Light of the World.

Now, here's what the father said on his deathbed, as reported in 1 Maccabees 2:49-50 (CEB), "Now the days drew near for Mattathias to die, and he spoke to his sons: 'Arrogance and contempt are present everywhere. It is a time of ruin and raging anger. Now, my children, demonstrate zeal for the Law, and give your lives for our ancestors' covenant.'" This is the beginning of the Zealots, who remain willing to die for God as martyrs.

There are three main reasons why the Zealot solution appeals to people in any generation. One, the motivation is political. People simply become sick of living under the oppression of a corrupt government. Two, the motivation is spiritual. God's people want to worship their God according to their convictions without interference from a godless government and reach a point where they refuse to endure any more interference and injustice. Three, the motivation is financial. The government makes decisions that weaken the economy and place heavy tax burdens on citizens for things that believers find appalling and refuse to continue paying for. Today, these motivations continue and make sense to those of us in America who are tired of paying for abortion clinics to stay open during COVID while churches were closed or paying for sick government schools who sexualize and mutilate children.

The question begging to be answered is this, "Does the New Testament have anyone who is a zealot?" The answer seems to be, yes. Acts 1:13 lists those present at the earliest days of the Church, "And when they had entered, they went up to the upper room, where they were staying, Peter and John and James and Andrew, Philip and

Thomas, Bartholomew and Matthew, James the son of Alphaeus and Simon the Zealot and Judas the son of James." A Bible commentary says,

> Simon the Zealot, as he is called here and in Luke 6:15, is called "Simon the Cananaean" in Mark 3:18 (followed by Matt. 10:4). "Cananaean" represents the Hebrew or Aramaic word corresponding to "Zealot" (from Gk. zēlōtēs). The word might denote Simon's zealous temperament, but Mark's retention of the untranslated Semitic word suggests that it is used as a technical term, denoting a member of the party of the Zealots.[54] The Zealots constituted the militant wing of the Jewish independence movement in the first century A.D.; it was they who took the lead in the revolt against Rome in A.D. 66.[55]

Some wonder if Jesus was put to death because the political and religious leaders thought His growing popularity could propel him to be a Zealot leader seeking to overthrow the government, which would create a massive backlash on all the Jews from the Roman government. As one Bible scholar says, "John attributes a political role and motive to the Sanhedrin, which fears that Jesus will cause unrest and stimulate the Romans to destroy the nation."[56]

Judas Iscariot, the "Dagger Man"

Admittedly, this is a debatable hypothesis, but some would say Judas Iscariot was a Zealot. If true, Judas was a corrupt man who was hoping that Jesus would rise up and lead an armed militia against the Roman government and then rule as its political leader. This hypothesis then suggests that, as soon as Judas realized Jesus was not going to be a political leader for the Zealots, he betrayed Him, having Jesus killed because He was of no political value. If true, Judas wanted to use Jesus for political reasons and had no interest in worshiping or obeying Him as Lord. Like most radicals, Judas would have thought that Jesus should fight with him or die by him.

Here's where things get interesting. Judas' last name, Iscariot, has a very telling meaning as it means "dagger" and refers to armed assassins and an "organized Jewish group who attempted to win freedom from the Romans. The word in Greek is derived from the Latin term *Sicarii* and literally means 'dagger men.' Josephus described them as hiding small daggers in their clothing, which they used in crowded situations to kill their victims."[57] A Bible dictionary says,

> SICARII [were a] group associated with revolt, robbery, and assassination. The Sicarii were known for hiding small, carved daggers in their clothes. In the ancient world, the term "Sicarii" could have applied to a range of people and groups but was most likely associated with political insurrection...About 600 Sicarii were involved in a revolt in Egypt...The New Testament refers to "Sicarii"...once, in Acts 21:38. The ESV translates...(sikarios) as "Assassins," as this group was known for their use of daggers and the speed of their executions...these small, concealable daggers apparently enabled them to strike anyone at any time.[58]

It goes on to speak of the writings of the respected ancient Jewish historian Josephus: "The Romans used the Latin word 'sicae' for daggers..."[59] Lastly, in the Roman Empire,

> although it is difficult to separate "Sicarii" from "robbers," the use of...(sikarios) in Acts 21:38 indicates a political agenda, not simply the theft of money and goods. Within the Roman Empire, some groups of politically and religiously motivated "robbers" complicate modern descriptions and one-word glosses. Both Mark 15:27 and Matt 27:38 use the word... (lēstēs) (leistes) for the robbers that hung on crosses beside Jesus. In Latin, these were called latrones...Based on the activities involved, the ancient concept of "robbers" could encompass four categories of meaning: bandits, rebels, rivals, and avengers...[60]

The Sicarii assassinated the high priest, Jonathan. They also assassinated other political leaders. People feared them for good reason. Among their ranks would have been former soldiers trained in battle, and many of the religious Sicarii shared a lot of political ideology with the Pharisees and the Essenes. A lot of their varied reactions may be attributable to personality, with the Pharisees freezing, the Essenes fleeing, and the Zealots fighting.

One thing the Zealots got wrong was a failure to understand the First and Second Comings of Jesus Christ. They only thought Jesus was returning once and expected Him to show up in glory instead of humility. When Jesus comes the second time, He will look a bit like a Sicarii. Revelation 19:11-16 says,

> Then I saw heaven opened, and behold, a white horse! The one sitting on it is called Faithful and True, and in righteousness he judges and

makes war. His eyes are like a flame of fire, and on his head are many diadems, and he has a name written that no one knows but himself. He is clothed in a robe dipped in blood, and the name by which he is called is The Word of God. And the armies of heaven, arrayed in fine linen, white and pure, were following him on white horses. From his mouth comes a sharp sword with which to strike down the nations, and he will rule them with a rod of iron. He will tread the winepress of the fury of the wrath of God the Almighty. On his robe and on his thigh he has a name written, King of kings and Lord of lords.

Revelation 5:5 describes Jesus as "the Lion of the tribe of Judah" as well as "the Lamb who was slain."[a] Pacifists tend to see Jesus only as Lamb, and Zealots tend to see Him only as Lion. The truth is, Jesus is both. Jesus is a Lamb with women and children throughout the Bible and will be a Lamb with His people in eternity. However, Jesus is a Lion with religious hypocrites in the Bible (especially the Pharisees and Sadducees) and will only be a Lion as He rules over His enemies in Hell forever. Jesus came the first time as a Lamb and is coming the second time as a Lion.

To the Zealots' credit, there is wisdom in carrying a weapon to protect yourself, your family, and other innocent people from such things as crimes and terrorist activities. The Second Amendment of the U.S. Constitution protects this right: "A well regulated Militia, being necessary to the security of a free State, the right of the people to keep and bear Arms, shall not be infringed."

In the physical realm, the sword refers to the

[a] Revelation 5:12, 13:8

right use of deadly force, capital punishment, and just war. Deadly force is when someone takes a human life to preserve another human life. It is self-defense against a sincere threat of harm or death. Capital punishment is the use of deadly force by the state, and it discourages anarchy, reduces vengeance, and stops the worst evildoers.

Just War

Our discussion of the Zealots raises the question of what causes a conflict or war to be "just." The following are commonly accepted guidelines by Christian scholars:
1. *Legitimate authority.* Mobs, terrorists, and anarchists are not legitimate authorities.
2. *Defensive, not offensive.* When Adolf Hitler ignited a world war by invading Poland, that was not a just war. Germany had not been provoked in any way. However, Poland's response to defend itself against Germany was just.
3. *Noble cause.* If human lives are going to be sacrificed, the cause must be worthwhile.
4. *Proportional force.* The response must be commensurate with the attack.
5. *Soldiers, not civilians, were targeted.* In a just war, the goal is to stop invading soldiers, not to punish innocent civilians.
6. *More lives are preserved than taken.* If sons and daughters are going to be sacrificed, then the cause must be virtuous, the benefit must outweigh the expenses, and more lives must be saved than lost.
7. *Last resort.* A just war begins with diplomacy and sanctions. If all those fail, then economic or military advancement ensues. Full military engagement is the last resort.

If a government has not become so corrupt that it needs to be overtaken, one other option for God's people is to carve out a subculture in which to live out their faith while largely maintaining distance from politics and the wider culture instead of seeking to overthrow the government. We will examine that next.

FINAL CHANCE FOR REAL RELIEF FOR A FARMER

CHAPTER 13
Should Christians Be a Separated Subculture Like the Ancient Pharisees?

Matthew 5:20 – For I tell you, unless your righteousness exceeds that of the scribes and Pharisees, you will never enter the kingdom of heaven.

The largest and most influential religious party in the days of Jesus Christ and the New Testament was the Pharisees, and they are mentioned roughly 100 times in the Bible.

Their two goals were simple: separation from the world and division from fellow believers they judged to be too worldly. Defining and defending these lines was much harder for the Pharisees than the Essenes, for one simple reason. While the Essenes retreated from the general culture, the Pharisees sought to remain in the culture, living in towns and cities with everyone else while carving out a distinct subculture of their very own.[61]

Ancient Fighting Fundamentalists

The spirit of the Pharisees continues today. When you see Christians online who have appointed themselves to judge and hold other

Christians "accountable," you are dealing with one of their spiritual descendants. When you see entire groups of Christians defining themselves by who and what fellow Christians they are against and declaring war over minor secondary issues, you have a modern-day Pharisee.

Today, these would be many of your Christian conservatives, traditionalists, and fundamentalists, as well as cessationists, who disbelieve in the ongoing work of the Holy Spirit and downplay the work of the demonic. In the name of holiness and purity, there is a group of believers in every generation wanting to separate not only from the world but from fellow Christians, even causing divisions between believers. They would say there is the world and there is the Church, and to stay pure, God's people must create significant separation and distance from the lost, fallen world. Being separated is what a Pharisee means – one who is separated. Modern-day Christian fundamentalism has, as one of its founding tenants, degrees of separation. It is literally built on the notion of the Pharisees. The thought is this: you need to have two degrees of separation. Whether you are actually a false teacher or apostate or I just think you're wrong and I'm concerned about you, I need to separate from you and then have two degrees of separation. This ensures that you don't have access to me to pollute, corrupt, or defile me. Practically, this means that if you have a relationship with someone and you don't think that they are apostate, but they are friends with someone who you think might be apostate, you need to shoot the apostate and the person who is associated with them. The result of such thinking is canceling them, even if they are fellow Christians.

In the New Testament, the Pharisees are probably the closest in theology to Jesus, but they are His most ardent enemies and opponents. They were a popular group, but Jesus became more popular; good old-fashioned jealousy is often the root trigger for a Pharisee spirit. Jesus also didn't appeal to them, and He wasn't approved by them. He didn't make it through their process to be considered acceptable for their conference, publishing house, seminary, or Bible college. They would confront, attack, and argue with Him. What he would not do is submit or surrender to them. Instead, He would publicly rebuke and sometimes even mock them.

The Pharisees were not the most educated, but they were the most influential. Generally, the Pharisees appealed to the poorer working class, wanted clarity, and did not like ambiguity. The Pharisees greatly disliked anything other than rigid answers to every question, so they decided to fill in what they perceived as gaps in God's Word with their own traditions, which led to ever-increasing legalisms. Jesus called them a brood of vipers and hypocrites repeatedly and publicly to warn others about their demonic and devout religion. The very people who were always demanding purity and accountability for everyone else were themselves impure and accountable to no one.

The fatal flaws of Pharisees yesterday and today are many, including the following:

One, they do not understand the difference between open-handed and closed-handed issues. While the progressive Sadducees wrongly put most everything in the open hand, the conservative Pharisees wrongly put most everything in the closed hand. Jesus called the closed-handed issues "weightier matters" in fighting with the Pharisees.[a] Paul speaks of what is of "first importance" as

[a] Matthew 23:23

opposed to things that are open-handed and of
secondary importance in 1 Corinthians 15:3 and
then goes on to speak of the gospel of Jesus Christ:
His life without sin, death for our sin, Resurrection
from the dead, and fulfillment of prophetic Old
Testament promises. Today, secondary or open-
handed matters would include such things as
the supernatural or sign spiritual gifts, age of
the earth, extent of the Flood, preferred Bible
translations, mode of baptism, or style of worship.
People who agree on closed-handed issues like
the Trinity, the Bible as God's Word, the Fall of
humanity into sin, the Person and work of Jesus
Christ, and the necessity of repentance of sin and
faith in Jesus Christ for salvation by grace through
faith can disagree on secondary issues without
dividing – something the spirit of the Pharisees
finds a reprehensible compromise.

Two, they assume they are always right, and those who disagree with them are always wrong. This, of course, leads to pride, arrogance, and a haughty spirit – things that the Bible makes clearer are sinful than the typical secondary things they attack fellow Christians for. This explains why they arrive on the scene over and over in the days of Jesus while He is teaching a crowd. Rather than coming to learn from Him, they make it their God-given mission to attack and correct Him for His errors and try to steal the crowd He gathered. The same thing happens online in our day.

Three, because they are devoted to separation, they publicly attack fellow believers they do not know without personally meeting with them to confirm what they believe. This leads to a lot of unnecessary character assassinations and creates a community where even the young novices in their freshman year at an unaccredited Bible college go online to critique lifelong Bible teachers. The Pharisees don't have a meal with Jesus; they pick fights with Jesus. They want to hold Jesus accountable and correct His "false" teaching. They do rules, not relationship. As a result, they tend to win arguments and not people because their focus is outward, not inward. Jesus criticizes the Pharisees for this very thing. In Matthew 23, He has a stinging series of rebukes and the whole chapter is Jesus giving seven woes, or curses, to the Pharisees. Generally, most of the curses are not because of things they're doing outwardly but inwardly. They're unloving, greedy, burden-giving, hypocritical, judgmental, non-relational, and proud, and they don't have life in the Spirit.

Four, they see themselves a bit like the drug dogs at the airport – sent by God to sniff out any false teaching, heresy, compromise, or wrong belief. They will call this a ministry of discernment, but often it is nothing more than a spirit of criticism. They fail to realize that just because someone disagrees with you does not mean they disagree with God. In one noteworthy example from John 9:13-41, the Pharisees critiqued Jesus for healing a blind man on the Sabbath. They failed to understand the difference between the letter of the law (that no work was to be done on the Sabbath) and the spirit of the law (that it was a gift of grace to bless God's people), and that healing a blind man on the Sabbath did not violate the spirit of the Sabbath laws. Paul, who was the most famous Pharisee before He met Jesus and understood the grace of God, said in Acts 26:5, "...according to the strictest party of our religion I have lived as a Pharisee." The Pharisees were the most hardcore of the most religious hardcore. They were intense, fierce, and disciplined, and no other group in their day could equal their intense religious demands. Jesus was not hardcore enough for them.

Five, perhaps the most fatal flaw with the Pharisees is that they had two lines of authority: the Torah (God's Scripture) and their own traditions. This led to a lot of conflict between what the Word of God says and what the teachers added to the Word of God. Today, we fall into the same trap when there is no distinction between principles and methods. The Bible gives us lots of singular and unchanging principles to be obeyed through multiple methods in every generation by wisdom and the leading of the Holy Spirit. The principles in the Bible are like the Torah: fixed and unchanging. When the methods, or our traditions and ways of living the Christian life, are considered as inflexible and unchanging as our principles, you get religious tradition and unnecessary infighting among Christians. Practically, this explains why there are a few hundred kinds of Baptists – they keep separating and dividing over traditions, methods, and secondary issues.

Father, Son, and Unholy Traditions

Underlying all the fatal flaws of Pharisees past and present is a downplaying of the work of the Holy Spirit. Their theological descendants today would, in large part, be not just the fundamentalists, but the fundamentalists who are cessationists. When you don't really, fully, and truly believe in the work of the Holy Spirit in someone, you nominate yourself for the job. You say, "I'm going to convict you, rebuke you, and control you. Read what I tell you, believe what I teach you, and follow my rules or endure my wrath."

What's interesting is that the Pharisees were not a formalized group. They didn't have a formal office in the government or within Judaism. Here's the big idea: they weren't under any authority; they were only in authority. Today, this is like the pajama Hadin online, spending day after day unnecessarily attacking genuine Christians. They include the discernment bloggers and the fool's parade of their followers, who demand everyone be accountable to them when they are accountable to no one. They even did this to Jesus Christ; they tried to cancel Him, and when that didn't work, they crucified Him.

Jerks Against Jesus

These kinds of religious people loved to publicly pick fights with Jesus. They would come to Him and argue over things like the Sabbath, fasting, tithing, food, purity, and divorce. The people don't love the Pharisees. They may fear them or even

respect them, but they don't love them. They love Jesus, and as a result, the Pharisees hate Him. They criticize Jesus for not listening to them and for being a friend of sinners. Again, we're back to the degrees of separation.

Jesus went to a party, and there were gals in clear heels and guys with neck tattoos who just got out of jail, smelling like cigarettes and Sodom. Seeing a parade of people with bad reputations heading into a home, the Pharisees assumed they were gathering to smoke weed, drink shots, fornicate, and intentionally violate every one of the 10 Commandments before sunrise. They assumed the worst of people. Because they did rules and not relationship, they didn't ask any of these people if they were instead, perhaps, going to a Bible study.

So, they accused Jesus of being a friend of sinners, a drunkard, and a glutton.[a] Those with the spirit of the Pharisees aren't beyond lying and character assassination, which helped kill Christ.

In addition, they make demands of Jesus, including performing a miracle. They even try to trap Jesus with the government about paying taxes, trying to lure Him into a legal battle. If you had to summarize the spirit of the Pharisees, it's the older brother syndrome.[b] When the younger brother gets grace, it's a disdain for him. When the party is thrown, and the father invites the two sons into the home, the older brother won't even enter because he is disgusted by grace. He's religious, he hates the rebellious, and he really hates when the rebellious gets grace.

The most famous Pharisee in the Bible, of course, is Saul, who becomes the apostle Paul.[c] If you want to see the heart of a Pharisee, just look at Saul before his conversion – harassing Christians and murdering Stephen – all in the name of being godly and obeying the Bible. That's the heart of Phariseeism, from the first century all the way to the present day. Paul says in Acts 23:6, "...I am a Pharisee, a son of Pharisees." So, it's multiple generations of legalism.

Today, as governments become less godly and more opposed to God and His people in the negative world, we can understand the frustration of the Pharisees, who were sick of trying to live out their faith under the rule of the godless yet powerful government of the Roman Empire. We can also admire their willingness to fight, pushing back against powerful forces in government and culture to preserve a necessary dividing line separating the Church from the world and maintaining the

[a] Matthew 11:19; Luke 7:34 [b] Luke 15:11-32 [c] Philippians 3

distinction between the two kingdoms. Their problem, however, was that they didn't know when to stop fighting. They fought with everyone over everything.

For those Christians who want to be involved politically and culturally, living as a subculture within the world system without compromising on the closed-handed issues of the Bible, the caution is to avoid the spirit of the Pharisees. In our day of the negative world, when Bible-believing Christians are seen as an immoral minority, it is unhelpful to have a group of Christians spending their time and energy attacking fellow Christians over secondary issues. When the government is trying to sexualize our children in schools, seize custody of our kids with mental health struggles to make them property of the state and mutilate their genitalia, and close churches and Christian schools, we need God's people to remain focused on the new battle lines threatening religious freedom in the home and Church. This includes conservative believers fighting with liberals who claim to be believers, something we will study next as we learn about the ancient Sadducees.

CHAPTER 14
Should Christians Become Progressive Like the Ancient Sadducees?

Matthew 16:6 – Jesus said to them, "Watch and beware of the leaven of the...Sadducees."

The great Protestant reformer Martin Luther once said, "Human nature is like a drunk peasant. Lift him into the saddle on one side, over he topples on the other side." If the Pharisees fell off the saddle onto the right side of the horse, the Sadducees fell off the saddle onto the left side of the horse.

If the Pharisees' goal was separatism, the Sadducees' goal was syncretism. Today, these "Christians" would be progressives or liberals. Some would be completely "woke," which is the counterfeit of being born again – flying rainbow flags on their churches where their lesbian pastor was ordained by their nonbinary bishop using their preferred pronouns. Others would be "soft woke," which is a Christian who seeks to keep one foot in the world and the other foot in the Church, unwilling to call things sinful for fear of having conflict or being unpopular. These are "evanjellyfish" with no spiritual vertebrae, and they tragically represent perhaps the majority of American Christians in churches who have been sensitive to seekers but insensitive to the Scriptures. Anytime the pursuit of "social justice" and making Heaven on earth for people supersedes a commitment to cosmic justice and people getting ready for Heaven by repenting of sin and receiving Jesus Christ as Lord and Savior, there is a replacing of the Church with the state and the use of the Church as a weaponized force for social and governmental change.

Roman Rainbow Flags

The spirit of the Sadducees today includes virtue signaling with words like love, which is bastardized to mean tolerance of sin, and "reconciliation" to try and reconcile together LGBTQIA, binary gender roles, woke progressive politics, and Christianity into one corrupt, compromised collective of reconciling light and darkness, the very thing God hates.[a]

The meaning behind the name Sadducees is not entirely clear, but it probably means "righteous" or "pure." For this group, being celebrated and tolerated by the world system for teaching tolerance of sin rather than repentance of sin is what they consider to be good behavior. They are a

Jewish party cited 14 times in the NT [New Testament], not referred to in the OT [Old Testament]. In the Gospel narrative they first appear together with Pharisees at John's baptism. He addressed them as "sons of snakes" and challenged them by asking, "Who said that you could escape the coming wrath of God?" He demanded that they show repentance

[a] Isaiah 5:20

in their lives and that they not make the idle boast that they were sons of Abraham (Mt 3:7-10). Later the Sadducees came along with some Pharisees to "test" Jesus, asking him to "show them a sign from heaven" (16:1). Jesus told his disciples, "Take heed and beware of the leaven of the Pharisees and Sadducees," and this is explained further as their "teaching" (vv. 6, 11, 12).[62]

One interesting fact is that the Pharisees and Sadducees didn't agree with one another. They had a lot of conflict, but they do come together on occasion to oppose and attack Jesus. The lesson here is don't be surprised when the Left and the Right come together to attack a common enemy.

I'll give you one weird example from my history some years ago. One week, I got picketed and protested by Westboro Baptist Church, the ancestors of the Pharisees. The next week, I got picketed and protested by some open and affirming universalistic, pro-gay "Christians," who are the sons and daughters of the Sadducees. Life is odd.

Jesus warns against the teaching of both the Pharisees on the Right and the Sadducees on the Left. It's a lot like our current political climate in America. Are you a Republican or a Democrat? Are you on the Right or the Left? Jesus says they both have some problems. Jesus' prayer and goal for His followers in that day were not that they would go right with the Pharisees or that they would go left with the Sadducees, but that they'd go up with the Kingdom of God and that the Spirit would come down to anoint them. We will examine this option later in the book.

The Sadducees demand a miracle from Jesus.[a]

[a] Matthew 16:1-4

149

They participate in the arrest of Peter and John. Oftentimes, the Sadducees are not the instigators because they're a small group. The Pharisees were much larger, more popular, louder, and well-known.

Whereas the Pharisees appealed to the masses, the Sadducees appealed to the elites. Political leaders, culture makers, and artistic creatives liked the Sadducees. They did not like the Pharisees. The Pharisees were the blue-collar majority. The Sadducees would be the creative, affluent, minority class. Today, they are artistic and innovative, pushing nonbinary storylines on children in entertainment and celebrating drag queen story hour at the local library. The ancient Jewish historian "Josephus states that the Sadducees did not have the support of the masses; they enjoyed only the 'confidence of the wealthy.'"[63]

Because they crave power and fame, when they see the apostles performing signs and wonders in Acts 5, they are "filled with jealousy," and they arrest and imprison them. This same spirit of the Sadducees continues today with Christian and pseudo-Christian influencers changing their beliefs and behaviors to increase followers and grow their platform while getting jealous and attacking others who seem to be succeeding at grabbing market share in their area of influence.

All the Cool Kids are Greek

The big commitment of the ancient Sadducees was promoting Hellenism, which was the popular syncretizing of Greek culture and philosophy with any and every nation and religion.

As bearers of the only monotheistic tradition before Christianity, Jews frequently faced the threat of extinction by generally more powerful polytheistic peoples, as attested in the Hebrew Bible. In that sense, the attractions, as well as the perceived dangers, of Hellenism were no different than earlier experiences with the Egyptians, Assyrians, Babylonians, or Persians. But Hellenism was also unique in that it incorporated a worldview and way of life that appeared to avoid the excesses and grossly unacceptable features of earlier outsiders and at the same time to offer cultural and economic advantages. As a result, this period saw unprecedented ruptures that decisively split families and pitted group against group—even among the priestly families.[64]

Much like the current worldview philosophies dominating culture and politics, such as deconstructionism and cultural Marxism, Hellenism and the imposition of pagan and sexually perverse Greek culture were popular and pervasive. The Sadducees were ancient liberals or progressives. Today, their spirit lives on in those who claim to be Christians while embracing ungodly and contradictory beliefs that deny orthodox faith rooted in the plain reading of the Scriptures. Following their attacks on Him, "Jesus responds by affirming the resurrection and accusing them of knowing neither the Scriptures nor the power of God (Mk 12:18–27 // Mt 22:23–33; Lk 20:27–38)."[65]

Josephus, the ancient Jewish historian, says, though this was a small group, they were the most difficult. They were the most contentious, unrelenting, rude, argumentative, and combative. They were impossible to deal with. We see this in their interactions with the Lord Jesus, including His arrest and crucifixion. "The Sadducees appear to have been important powerbrokers at the center of Judean politics, part of the religious elite who affirmed the status quo. It is best to refer to them as a religio-political 'party' within first-century A.D. Judaism (where religion and politics were inseparable)."[66]

Because the Sadducees had more fame, power, and money in secular culture and government than other religious groups, they also largely controlled the Sanhedrin.

The Sanhedrin in Jerusalem, as it appears in the gospels, Josephus, and rabbinic literature, has been understood alternately as the high priests' political council, the highest legislative body in Jewish Palestine, the supreme judicial court, the grand jury for important cases, the council of the Pharisaic school, and the final court of appeals in deciding halakic questions.[67]

The apostate Jewish Sanhedrin, working with the pagan Roman government, conspired together to kill Christ. The Romans did this to preserve state worship of their emperor, and the Sadducees did this to increase the power and wealth gotten from their unholy alliance with the Roman government.

The Gospels reveal that in Mark and Matthew the Sanhedrin condemns Jesus to death (Mark 14:64; Matt 26:66), but then must approach the Roman governor to have Jesus executed...John attributes a political role and motive to the Sanhedrin, which fears that Jesus will cause unrest and stimulate the Romans to destroy the nation (11:48–50). Luke, a gentile Christian, describes the Sanhedrin as if it were a typical Hellenistic-Roman city council: "The elders-council...of the people gathered together, both chief priests and scribes, and led him away to their Sanhedrin" (22:66).[68]

Curiously, one thing that the Pharisees and Sadducees share is trying to boss Jesus around. The Sadducees are mentioned some 15 times in the New Testament, usually in conflict with Christ or the apostles. They are not mentioned as often as the Pharisees in conflict with Jesus likely because their group was smaller, and they were generally less aggressive. Josephus mentions them six times, and the ancient rabbinic literature also mentions them. Here's the big idea: if the Pharisees over-contended and under-contextualized, the Sadducees over-contextualized and under-contended. They got way too deep into the culture and way too shallow into Scripture. They were upstream in culture with great influence and, because they were chameleons, became popular in most social circles. They are today's left-leaning, politically motivated, culturally approved "Christians" marching in anti-police protests, supporting same-sex marriage, pressuring politicians to not support the nation of Israel, and turning the pages of the Bible into an origami exercise to justify abortion, gender confusion, and sexual sin.

Red-Letter Losers

The beliefs of the Sadducees are curiously

amiss. They did not accept all the Scriptures. The Pharisees had Torah plus tradition by adding to God's Word. On the other side of the continuum, the Sadducees removed parts of the Bible that did not agree with their compromise with culture. Today, this would include "red-letter Christians" that ignore all of what the Bible says, except for the words of Jesus, not understanding that all Scripture is "God breathed,"[a] and the "word of Christ"[b] and the entire Old Testament was the Bible that Jesus learned and taught. Furthermore, Jesus talked about God flooding the earth in the days of Noah, the destruction of Sodom and Gomorrah for sexual sin, and quoted Genesis' command that marriage is solely for a man and a woman. The red-letter Christians don't even believe the red letters.

There were entire books of the Bible that the Sadducees just got rid of, including all of Daniel. Anything that mentioned the Resurrection, Heaven and Hell, eternal life, angels, miracles, demons, or the supernatural was omitted. They were like Thomas Jefferson, who sat down in the White House, cut out the parts of the Bible he didn't like, and came up with what he called *The Philosophy of Jesus of Nazareth*.

The Sadducees, ancient and modern, really hate the Bible's emphasis on the Fall and human sin. They didn't agree that human beings were totally depraved, with sin infecting and affecting all their being. Like modern progressives, they wrongly believed people were good and making progress at getting better and better. Like liberals of every age, they wrongly trusted time and education to cause moral progress because they thought we are all basically good people.

[a] 2 Timothy 3:16 [b] Romans 10:17

Also offensive to the Sadducees was God's sovereignty and providential ruling over the affairs of mankind. Instead, they downplayed God's sovereignty and stressed our free will in human decision-making. For them, the thought of being under authority, including God's, was repugnant.

In addition, they were morally and culturally progressive, and they wanted to emphasize tolerance over repentance. One thing the Pharisees do get right is that people need to repent of sin, but they didn't repent of their personal sin. What the Sadducees got wrong was that they practiced tolerance over repentance. If you were Greek in your behavior, which included your sexual progressivism or your philosophical syncretism, they would tolerate that. They tolerated lots of transgenderism and sexual sin, just like liberal "Christians" today.

They also did not have a clear, singular leader. It was more of an ideology or leaderless movement. It was an upstream, progressive vision saying, "What if we took some of the moral beliefs out of the Bible and erased the sovereignty of God and the sinfulness of man? What if we took out the supernatural parts that we don't like and changed it from a story of good news about what Jesus has done to good deeds and what we can do to make the world a better place because we are good people?" This was ancient, godless social justice activism, just like today.

Sadducees also practiced deconstruction. This is the classic effort of the Left, and it started all the way in Genesis 3. When Satan showed up to our first parents, he just asked a question, but the question was aimed at deconstruction. "Did God actually say...?"ᵃ He's trying to dismantle,

ᵃ Genesis 3:1

156

or deconstruct, everything God has constructed. In postmodernism and Critical Theory in the present day, it's based upon that same spirit of deconstruction. The way the Sadducees would practice deconstruction, especially when they were publicly attacking Jesus, was by asking leading questions seeking to deconstruct everything He had constructed and taught. These are the people who don't build things; they break things. They're not participating in traditional theory, which creates; they're engaging in Critical Theory, which destroys. This is not the building crew; this is the demo crew. If you would like to learn more about this, I wrote an entire book called *Christian Theology vs. Critical Theory*.

In addition, they were apostate heretics, and they had an over-realized eschatology, wrongly believing that people working together in a sort of globalist vision could create Heaven on earth without Jesus returning. One of the things they denied was the resurrection of the dead. This was the big conflict point between the Pharisees and Sadducees. The Sadducees denied resurrection, and, as a result, there's no Heaven, there's no Hell, and there's no eternal judgment. All you've got is this life; you're not really a sinner, and God's not really sovereign. What you need to do is be a good person, make good decisions, and make the world a better place. They were known for being combative, argumentative, self-righteous, and given to cancel culture. Anyone who disagrees with the spirit of the Sadducees, yesterday or today, is attacked and ignored for being out of touch, outdated, primitive, unlearned, uncouth, repressive, intolerant, bigoted, and behind the times.

Acts 23:8 says, "For the Sadducees say that there is no resurrection, nor angel, nor spirit, but the Pharisees acknowledge them all." That's the progressive Left today, including the apostate mainline liberal Protestant denominations. Angels, demons – that's crazy talk. Heaven and Hell – you people are nuts. All we have is one life. We need to save the planet. We need to build a utopian society. We need to be good people. We all need to get along. We need to tolerate each other. We need to allow the culture to edit our religious beliefs. We need to get rid of those outdated, primitive, bigoted parts of the Bible so that we can make room for the best of human culture by getting rid of those shameful ancient tales about the moral monster called God.

Pathetic Progressives

Today, we would call these folks "woke" or progressive. They skip church to march in Black Lives Matter protests. They're flying the rainbow flag, and it's not because they are big fans of the Noahic Covenant. They probably even wore medical masks at some point to virtue signal during flu season. They're always finding ways to publicly show that they are morally superior and more advanced, educated, and progressive, as if that were a good thing. What drove the hearts of the Sadducees continues to this day. They want to be social influencers. They want to get their photo taken with the most famous, rich, and influential people.

Today, the media and social platforms are controlled by the descendants of the Sadducees. They are not Bible-believing, even if they say they are Christians. The result is that they will throttle anyone and anything that agrees with all of Scripture, but they will highlight and advance anyone who says they are a Christian while opposing what the Bible says. The way to become

famous in that day and our day is the same: say you believe in God and then misquote Scripture, encouraging people to sin against God while being hailed as moral examples.

There was a book written some years ago by Dr. Drew Pinsky, a psychiatrist for celebrities. He did not seem to be a Christian when I co-hosted his call-in radio show or appeared on his television show with my wife. A book he wrote called *The Mirror Effect*, after working with celebrities in addiction for much of his adult life, says the problem with social media is this: celebrities model behavior, and followers then mirror the behavior of the celebrities. So, if you want to be an influencer, a celebrity, or well-known, like the

Sadducees, you need to model beliefs or behaviors that are outlandish outliers. Why? Because if you just say what everybody else says and you do what everybody else does, nobody pays attention to you; you're not interesting. However, if you act crazy, everyone starts talking about you and following you; then you become famous, or at least infamous. Quickly, however, your followers start saying and doing the same crazy things, and, to remain relevant, you need to become more wildly unhinged to keep them interested in the self-destructive reality television show slow motion car wreck that is your life. This cycle continues over and over as celebrities model increasingly unhealthy behavior and their followers mirror it, which explains why pretty much every study confirms that the more time people spend on social media, the worse their mental health is. This is exactly the heart of the Sadducees. They just kept pushing the bounds of what was outlandish until it became normal. Some of you might ask, "How much darker can this world go? How much weirder can people be? How much stranger can celebrities become?" The answer is that there's no bottom.

Tragically, this is a counterfeit of the worship of God. God is supposed to model for us, and we are supposed to mirror Him. When the Bible says we were made in God's "image" and "likeness," it means we are to be a mirror that reflects Him to the world[a], just like Jesus Christ, who is the perfect "image of...God."[b] We were made to mirror, and when we do not mirror God, we find someone else to be our idol, and we mirror them instead. We are to look up to Jesus. He models for us, and we are to mirror Him. What the Sadducees wanted was to be influencers; they wanted to be celebrities; they

[a] Genesis 1:26, 5:3 [b] Colossians 1:15

wanted to be like Jesus lifted up in glory for all to see and imitate. The ancient Sadducees took Greek culture, syncretized it with Scripture, and created what looks a lot like progressive, woke, apostate Christianity today.

This political and cultural option is not possible for any true Christian. This thinking erases the line between the Church and the world by reducing or removing the Word of God to promote the tolerance of sin over the repentance of sin. Furthermore, it denies the existence of the two kingdoms and leads to syncretism and then apostasy. The question remains: How would Jesus vote? We will answer this question in the final chapter.

CHAPTER 15
How Would Jesus Vote?

John 18:36 – Jesus answered, "My kingdom is not of this world..."

Today, most every religion, spirituality, philosophy, social justice cause, and political party attempts to find ways to pull Jesus Christ into their group. Why? Because He is the most influential person in the history of the world. More songs have been sung to Him, more books written regarding Him, and more lives devoted to Him than anyone who has lived in the history of the world.

As Jesus' fame grew in the first century, along with the growing movement of the Christian Church in His wake, you would expect Christ and Christians to join one of the four parties we've studied. However, Christ and Christians did no such thing.

The Sadducean option totally subordinated the things of God to the state. The Roman government appointed and controlled the Jewish high priest at will. Second, there was the Essene approach of withdrawal from society to await messianic intervention. A third approach was that of the Zealots who openly revolted against Rome. They relied on the sword and expected divine intervention on their behalf. Finally, there was the Pharisaic option. They lived in the world but tried to be separate from it by adhering to rules that covered externals. Jesus rejected all of these options.[69]

"Instead, he was in the world but not of it. Unlike the Pharisees, his separation was not merely external. He rejected the philosophies and values of the world in favor of heavenly principles, but that kept him neither from proclaiming the gospel nor from meeting people's needs."[70]

Heaven
Church
Bible

World
Hell

Imagine the pressure that would be on Jesus Christ around election time if He were walking on the earth today. Imagine the constant pressure from all sides to join a political party and use His fame to attack the other political parties. There was incredible pressure on Christ to join a party, compromise some aspect of His convictions, and enjoy the benefits that come from not standing alone and being shot from all sides. However, Jesus Christ came not to join a party but to start a new party called the Church of Jesus Christ, which brought a new opportunity to go up and down instead of forward or backward (Zealots and Essenes) or right or left (Pharisees and Sadducees). This fifth and final group is the Christians. Christianity emerged in a negative world, ruled over by a godless Roman government and surrounded by a demonic culture of Greek perversion and gender confusion. The Church was launched and grew in the same tension we face today: the tug-of-war pulling between the Pharisees on the right, the Sadducees on the left, the Zealots going forward into conflict, and the Essenes going backwards into retreat.

Pick Your Party

If you were to pick between the four parties – Zealots or Essenes, Pharisees or Sadducees – which would you choose? How you answer that question is influenced by a few things.

One, what government are you under? How bad is that government compared to all the awful regimes God's people have suffered under in the Scriptures and history?

Two, what is your personality? If you tend

toward fight, your tendency will be toward a Zealot or a Pharisee, and if your tendency is toward flight, you will likely be a Sadducee or Essene.

Three, what life stage are you in? As a young man, I would have gravitated toward being a Zealot or Pharisee, ready to fight and push back, unafraid of conflict and criticism. I could never be a Sadducee, as I have better odds of becoming pregnant than a liberal. However, now that I'm a grandpa, if the government and culture began collapsing around me, I would want to do all I could to get my wife, kids, and grandchildren out of harm's way, so I'd probably choose the Essene path.

The paths people take are often largely influenced by who they are, when and where they live, the relationships they value, and what experiences have shaped them. No matter what, God's people should go up before they go forward, backward, left, or right.

According to the storyline of the Bible, there was a war in Heaven that came to earth. King Jesus has come down to earth and will again come down one last time, bringing the Kingdom in His wake to push the devil and his demons down to Hell forever. Every day of our existence on earth, we are living amidst a great battle that has been raging since long ago in Heaven. Each day, our decisions either invite Heaven down or pull Hell up into our lives. This includes our politics.

Jesus' half-brother, James, used binary thinking, urging Christians not to pull Hell up into our lives through popular and prevalent living, which is "false to the truth...earthly, unspiritual, demonic... and...vile," but instead to invite Heaven down into our lives with the "wisdom from above."[a]

[a] James 3:14-17

Paul instructed, "Set your minds on things that are above, not on things that are on earth."[a] Jesus taught us to pray and then live Heaven down, not Hell up, saying, "Your kingdom come, your will be done, on earth as it is in heaven."[b] When we see the Spirit fall on people in the Bible and to this day, this is living "Kingdom down" rather than "culture up."

To be a faithful Christian, living in the two kingdoms with loyalty to the Kingdom of God but love for our nation, is admittedly complicated. As a Christian, conservative Republican, I cannot, for example, overlook the growing concerns I have with my own political party because I am loyal to the Bible and gospel ministry calling for the repentance of sin, even when it is committed by pro-family and pro-life candidates that I share more in common with than their progressive opponents. Repentance of sin is regardless of political party. Additionally, Gallup polling has reported that 55% of Republicans now support gay marriage, something a Bible-believing Christian cannot agree with.[71]

3 Commands for Christians

For Christians, we must think long-term instead of short-term. Forever and ever, we will be in the Kingdom of God. For a short life that the Bible calls a "vapor" in comparison, we will be on earth under the rule of a government that is flawed. Our hope must be to not just recruit people to our politics but also evangelize people to our Savior. All the nations and governments of the world are coming to an end and will be replaced by the rule of Jesus Christ as King of Kings and Lord of Lords

[a] Colossians 3:2 [b] Matthew 6:5-15

forever. For this reason, to keep thinking and serving north and south, Kingdom down instead of Hell up, we must proclaim the gospel to all political parties. Acts 17:30-31 says, "he commands all people everywhere to repent, because he has fixed a day on which he will judge the world in righteousness by a man whom he has appointed; and of this he has given assurance to all by raising him from the dead." To live Kingdom down and gospel-focused requires at least three things.

One, the Word goes over the world. Whatever your political, cultural, or social thoughts are, the Word judges the world. This includes your politics.

Two, Christ is over your cause. If you speak and serve Christ, you will have a heart for various causes. You'll care about the unborn, the raped, the trafficked, and the victim. Since people are made in the image of and loved by God, if you're for Christ, you're going to have some causes. But what happens is this: groups tend to put their cause over Christ. The way things go astray is if you have Christ and a cause side-by-side. The cause can be anything, including good things like adopting kids, digging wells, feeding the hungry, ending sex trafficking, or getting kids out of foster care into permanent homes. All great ideas. However, the problem is, which is your priority – the cause, or Christ? If Christ remains your priority, you will have causes, but your primary cause is Christ. If your cause becomes your priority, you're now using Christ for your cause. You're not loving and worshiping Christ; you're using Christ. And so, for the early Church, that's why they said that Jesus Christ is Lord. This means that over our politics and over our cause is our Christ.

Three, preach repentance over tolerance. Today, a faithful Christian leader must call the Sadducees to repent of their progressivism, the

Pharisees to repent of their legalism, the Zealots to repent of their bitterness, and the Essenes to repent of their indifference or even cowardice. The gospel calls every group to repent of sin, trust in Christ, and form a new group that doesn't always go forward, backward, left, or right but seeks to always go up to the Lord Jesus Christ as the Holy Spirit comes down. When the first Christians were called "the Way,"[a] it was because the Church was following a new way to live patterned after Jesus Christ, who said He was also "the way."[b]

The problem with the Pharisees was that they were not converting people. The problem with the Sadducees was that they were not converting people. The problem with the Zealots was that they were converting people to their political party but not to their God. And the problem with the Essenes was that they didn't even know lost people, so they couldn't convert people. The early Church focused on missions and evangelism, reaching people and planting churches over the various alternatives like syncretism, sectarianism, anarchy, or isolation. Here's what happened as a result: the early Church contended better than the Pharisees, contextualized better than the Sadducees, did community better than the Essenes, and affected more global change than the Zealots.

Each of these four groups wanted something. The Pharisees want purity. They'd say you're not pure unless you're committed to Christ first and foremost. The Sadducees would say they wanted to be relevant. Here's the big idea: We don't make Christianity or the Bible relevant. We assume that it is, and we show the relevance of Christ in the Bible. The Zealots would say they wanted to affect change, but you will do that through the preaching

[a] Acts 9:2 [b] John 14:6

169

of the gospel of Jesus Christ because the deepest change is new life at the soul level. God saves people, and when the Holy Spirit is poured out, institutions are changed. For the Essenes, their motto was, "We just want to have a loving, safe community." You can only have that if the gospel is at the center.

In every ministry, including your church, there are Pharisees, Sadducees, Essenes, and Zealots, along with just plain old Christians. In every ministry, there are these four groups that are constantly pulling on the leadership. If you love Jesus and you're trying to be faithful, you're caught in the middle, and you're feeling it on the local level every election season. One day, you're feeling pulled to the left by the Sadducees, and the

next day, you're feeling pulled to the right by the Pharisees. The next day, something breaks in the news, and you're feeling pulled into conflict and anger by the Zealots. The day after that, something else breaks in the news that seems overwhelming, and you feel pulled into retreat and isolation like the Essenes. Christians must maintain their position under the authority of God, filled with the Spirit of God, and integrous to the Word of God. You will constantly live in this tension and pressure point between these four groups. Again, the key is to maintain your position: don't go forward, backward, left, or right. Go up and find your King Jesus and His Kingdom, and invite the Holy Spirit down to allow you to be faithful to Him in all of life.

In addition, do not be surprised when these various groups align to attack you. These groups are not mutually exclusive. We see this, for example, when the Pharisees and Sadducees, who hate each other, come together to attack Jesus. They find a common enemy. For ministry leaders, don't be shocked when one of these groups idolizes you for a decision you make or what you preach. Soon, the same people who idolized you will eventually demonize you. That's exactly what Judas, if he was a Zealot, did to Jesus. He idolized Him, and when he didn't get what he wanted, he demonized Him.

The reason there is pressure to go forward, backward, left, or right and join a party is so that the group can put their stamp of approval on you, welcome you into their group, defend you against the other groups, and reward you for the work you do. This is not always bad, but sometimes it is a counterfeit of God's anointing. Rather than waiting for God to put His blessing on us, we settle for some religious or political group to admit or endorse us. You have two choices: you can receive their approval or His anointing. However, if you choose any of these four groups without first seeking the Kingdom, like Jesus says, He will not anoint you because you're not supposed to be on their team but His team, which calls all teams to repentance of sin and loyalty to one King. This is a prophetic position – outside of the mainstream, a voice calling out in the wilderness. The prophetic place can be lonely, misunderstood, and frustrating, but it is also faithful to what Jesus told us – that the world will sometimes hate us, reject us, and not speak well of us.

Let me also tell you this: as a Christian, you need to endure a lot of pain. You're going to be treated poorly, you're going to be hated, some people are going to trash you, they're going to turn against you, they're going to falsely accuse you, they're going to post negative things online, and they're going to cause you great fear. It's going to hurt like hell, but it's all for Heaven. You can either have their approval or His anointing, but most of the time, you can't have both.

My encouragement would be not to settle for their approval but to remain in His anointing. It's the most important thing you have, and it can get you through whatever you must endure. Along the way, have a patriotic love for your nation and do your best to vote like Jesus, which we will further study next in the conclusion to this book.

CONCLUSION
Plug Your Nose and Vote

Ecclesiastes 10:2 (NIV) – The heart of the wise inclines to the right, but the heart of the fool to the left.

I consider myself a Christian, conservative, and Republican in that order. As a Christian, my first and highest loyalty is to my Lord and Savior, Jesus Christ. Furthermore, as a Christian, I believe that most of our national and cultural issues are, at their root, spiritual issues. Until people turn from sin and trust in Jesus Christ as Savior and live under His lordship in authority over every inch of their lives, born again and empowered by the Holy Spirit, the Fall and curse will continue to pull everyone and everything down, because sin is like gravity. It is because of these convictions that my first commitment is to Christian ministry, Bible teaching, and the preaching of the gospel of Jesus Christ.

As a conservative, I care about issues such as religious freedom, pro-family policies that encourage men and women to marry and raise children, school choice for parents to decide the best way to educate their children, small government that does not encroach on personal liberties, a reduction in taxes along with national spending and debt, secure borders to ensure safety for citizens, support of the nation of Israel, commitment to appointing conservative Supreme Court justices, and opposition to the holocaust of abortion, which is perennially the leading cause of death. Because I am a Christian conservative, I find myself further to the right than the modern-day Republican Party on many issues. However, when left with the binary choice between being a Democrat or Republican, I would have to forsake considerably more of my Bible-based convictions to be a Democrat than a Republican, and so I am a Republican.

Regarding candidates, I find it important to consider if they can actually do their job. For example, since the President of the United States of America has a job of unimaginable importance and stress, their fitness for the job must be considered. It's one thing to win an election, and it's an entirely different thing to govern, lead, and do the job effectively. Subsequently, a political leader must have the physical, mental, and emotional stamina to stay in the fight day after day, pressing ahead no matter what the obstacle.

Regarding voting, I would encourage you to look at policies more than personalities. In our celebrity age, with constant bombardment from all sides via the interconnectedness of the internet, more than any time in world history, we have a voyeuristic ability to peer into the private details of people's lives that is frankly unholy and unhealthy if we believe anything about the Bible's forbidding of gossiping and busy bodying. The result is that we lose sight of policies and get caught up in personalities – whether we like someone or not and whether we respect and support what they stand for. The truth is, people and their personalities come and go, but their policies remain. This means sensible voters should not overlook people and their character, but since we are voting for someone to do things other than be our friend, policies should drive our decision-making. When it comes to voting, you have a few options:

1. You can choose not to vote and remove yourself from the process entirely, as Christian Anabaptists do.

2. You can cast a protest vote for a candidate who supports your policies but has no chance of actually winning and do so as a personal moral statement to lose with a clear conscience.

3. You can plug your nose and vote for a candidate who has a chance of winning. Admittedly, for Christians, the choices we are given are often not the people we want. Until Jesus returns, we will not have a political leader we are completely proud of, and, until then, I would encourage you to plug your nose and vote if this is how you feel.

ENDNOTES

1. https://www.firstthings.com/article/2022/02/the-three-worlds-of-evangelicalism
2. https://virginiahistory.org/learn/george-washingtons-farewell-address#:~:text=%E2%80%9COf%20all%20the%20dispositions%20and,men%20and%20citizens
3. Patrick Henry, "'And I Don't Care What It Is': The Tradition-History of a Civil Religion Proof-Text," Journal of the American Academy of Religion 49, issue 1 (March 1981): 41.
4. https://www.persecution.org/2024/02/15/young-adults-in-the-uk-open-to-bible-ban/
5. E. L. Johnson, "Apostasy," ed. David G. Benner and Peter C. Hill, Baker Encyclopedia of Psychology & Counseling, Baker Reference Library (Grand Rapids, MI: Baker Books, 1999), 91.
6. Ibid., 92.
7. Michael J. Smith., "The Failure of the Family in Judges, Part 2: Samson," Bibliotheca Sacra 162 (2005): 424.
8. P. R. Gilchrist, "Government," ed. Geoffrey W Bromiley, The International Standard Bible Encyclopedia, Revised (Wm. B. Eerdmans, 1979–1988), 546.
9. Wayne Grudem, Christian Ethics: An Introduction to Biblical Moral Reasoning (Wheaton, IL: Crossway, 2018), 434.
10. Ibid.
11. Walter A. Elwell and Barry J. Beitzel, "Theocracy," Baker Encyclopedia of the Bible (Grand Rapids, MI: Baker Book House, 1988), 2049.
12. E. A. Judge, "In the New Testament," ed. D. R. W. Wood et al., New Bible Dictionary (Leicester, England; Downers Grove, IL: InterVarsity Press, 1996), 431.
13. P. R. Gilchrist, "Government," ed. Geoffrey W Bromiley, The International Standard Bible Encyclopedia, Revised (Wm. B. Eerdmans, 1979–1988), 546.

14. Wayne Grudem, Christian Ethics: An Introduction to Biblical Moral Reasoning (Wheaton, IL: Crossway, 2018), 471–472.
15. For the wording of the Mayflower Compact, see www.historyplace.com/unitedstates/revolution/mayflower.htm. For primary source background on the Mayflower Compact, see http://mayflowerhistory.com/primary-sources-and-books/.)
16. Freedom in the World: 2015," Freedom House, https://freedomhouse.org/sites/default/files/01152015_FIW_2015_final.pdf.)
17. The exact figure is 4,101,291,986 people out of the world population of 7,349,472,254 as of Aug. 11, 2016. See "Number of World Citizens Living under Different Regimes," Our World in Data, https://ourworldindata.org/grapher/world-pop-by-political-regime
18. Wayne Grudem, Christian Ethics: An Introduction to Biblical Moral Reasoning (Wheaton, IL: Crossway, 2018), 463–464.
19. Rodney Stark, The Victory of Reason: How Christianity Led to Freedom, Capitalism, and Western Success (New York: Random House, 2005), 28.
20. https://speculaprincipum.substack.com/p/a-primer-on-state-constitutions
21. https://www.repository.law.indiana.edu/cgi/viewcontent.cgi?article=3247&context=facpub#:~:text=1%20The%20Fourteenth%20Amendment%20has,information%20or%20freedom%20of%20worship.
22. https://www.britannica.com/topic/Cantwell-v-Connecticut
23. https://berkleycenter.georgetown.edu/cases/lemon-v-kurtzman--2
24. https://www.uscourts.gov/educational-resources/educational-activities/first-amendment-and-religion
25. https://christianhistoryinstitute.org/magazine/article/baptist-liberties-and-the-wall-of-separation
26. William Arndt et al., A Greek-English Lexicon of the New Testament and Other Early Christian Literature (Chicago: University of Chicago Press, 2000), 356.

27. D. Edmond Hiebert, "Selected Studies from Jude Part 1: An Exposition of Jude 3–4," Bibliotheca Sacra 142 (1985): 144.

28. G. F. C. Fronmüller, "The Epistle General of Jude," in Lange's Commentary on the Holy Scriptures, with additions by J. Isidor Mombert (Grand Rapids: Zondervan Publishing House, n.d.), p. 13.

29. D. Edmond Hiebert, "Selected Studies from Jude Part 1: An Exposition of Jude 3–4," Bibliotheca Sacra 142 (1985): 144.

30. Warren W. Wiersbe, The Bible Exposition Commentary, vol. 2 (Wheaton, IL: Victor Books, 1996), 548.

31. Frank Stagg, "Rendering to God What Belongs to God: Christian Disengagement from the World," J Ch St 18 (Spring 1976): 217–218.

32. John S. Feinberg and Paul D. Feinberg, Ethics for a Brave New World (Wheaton, IL: Crossway Books, 1993), 396–397.

33. https://www.templetonprize.org/laureate-sub/solzhenitsyn-acceptance-speech/

34. Kennedy and Newcombe. What if Jesus Had Never Been Born?, 70.

35. https://newhouse.syracuse.edu/news/survey-of-journalists-provides-insights-into-the-state-of-journalism-today/

36. https://archaeology.co.uk/articles/opinion/babylon.htm

37. https://home.treasury.gov/policy-issues/international/g-7-and-g-20#:~:text=The%20G%2D7%2C%20which%20includes,and%20central%20bank%20governor%20level.

38. https://www.foxnews.com/politics/nearly-half-all-us-governors-urge-drastic-change-global-health-organization-before-new-pandemic-hits

39. https://heritage.humanists.uk/humanist-manifesto-ii-1973/#:~:text=The%20ultimate%20goal%20should%20be,and%20global%20measures%20will%20suffice.

40. https://www.pewresearch.org/short-

reads/2022/12/08/about-four-in-ten-u-s-adults-believe-humanity-is-living-in-the-end-times/
41. https://www.acton.org/research/lord-acton-quote-archive
42. https://oll.libertyfund.org/quote/lord-acton-writes-to-bishop-creighton-that-the-same-moral-standards-should-be-applied-to-all-men-political-and-religious-leaders-included-especially-since-power-tends-to-corrupt-and-absolute-power-corrupts-absolutely-1887
43. https://about-history.com/list-of-dictatorships-by-death-toll-the-top-10-biggest-killers-in-history/
44. Derek R. Brown, 2 Thessalonians, ed. Douglas Mangum, Lexham Research Commentaries (Bellingham, WA: Lexham Press, 2013), 2 Th 2:1–17.
45. Cynthia Long Westfall, "Roman Religions and the Imperial Cult," ed. John D. Barry et al., The Lexham Bible Dictionary (Bellingham, WA: Lexham Press, 2016).
46. Tommas Pace, "Crime," ed. John D. Barry et al., The Lexham Bible Dictionary (Bellingham, WA: Lexham Press, 2016.
47. James M. Freeman and Harold J. Chadwick, Manners & Customs of the Bible (North Brunswick, NJ: Bridge-Logos Publishers, 1998), 294.
48. Cf. T. Austad, 'Eivind Berggrav and the Church of Norway's Resistance Against Nazism, 1940–1945', Mid-Stream XXVI, no. 1 (1987), pp. 51–61.
49. Torleiv Austad, "Attitudes towards the State in Western Theological Thinking," Themelios 16, no. 1 (1990): 20.
50. G. W. Buchanan, "Essenes," ed. Geoffrey W. Bromiley, The International Standard Bible Encyclopedia, Revised (Wm. B. Eerdmans, 1979–1988), 150.
51. https://www.newworldencyclopedia.org/entry/Juche
52. Ibid.
53. Miller, S. R. (1994). Vol. 18: Daniel. The New American Commentary (312–313). Nashville: Broadman & Holman Publishers.
54. Gk. ζηλωτής, Heb. qannā'i, Aram. qan' anā'. The Zealots were the spiritual heirs of the Hasmonaean

insurgents of the second century B.C., who rose in response to the call of Mattathias: "Whoever is zealous (ζηλῶν) for the law and supports the covenant, let him come out with me!" (1 Macc. 2:27). Mattathias in turn acted in the spirit of Elijah, who was "very zealous (ζηλῶν ἐζήλωκα) for Yahweh, the God of hosts" (1 Kings 19:10), and earlier still of Phinehas, who "was zealous (ἐζήλωσεν) for his God" (Num. 25:13). Cf. 21:20.

55. F. F. Bruce, The Book of the Acts, The New International Commentary on the New Testament (Grand Rapids, MI: Wm. B. Eerdmans Publishing Co., 1988), 40–41.

56. Anthony J. Saldarini, "Sanhedrin," ed. David Noel Freedman, The Anchor Yale Bible Dictionary (New York: Doubleday, 1992), 977.

57. Chad Brand et al., eds., "Assassins," Holman Illustrated Bible Dictionary (Nashville, TN: Holman Bible Publishers, 2003), 133.

58. David H. Wenkel, "Sicarii," ed. John D. Barry et al., The Lexham Bible Dictionary (Bellingham, WA: Lexham Press, 2016).

59. David H. Wenkel, "Sicarii," ed. John D. Barry et al., The Lexham Bible Dictionary (Bellingham, WA: Lexham Press, 2016).

60. David H. Wenkel, "Sicarii," ed. John D. Barry et al., The Lexham Bible Dictionary (Bellingham, WA: Lexham Press, 2016).

61. To learn more about the Pharisees, see Everett Ferguson, Backgrounds of Early Christianity, 2nd ed. (Grand Rapids, MI: William B. Eerdmans Publishing Company, 1993).

62. Walter A. Elwell and Barry J. Beitzel, "Sadducees," Baker Encyclopedia of the Bible (Grand Rapids, MI: Baker Book House, 1988), 1880.

63. Gary G. Porton, "Sadducees," ed. David Noel Freedman, The Anchor Yale Bible Dictionary (New York: Doubleday, 1992), 894.

64. Leonard J. Greenspoon, "Hellenism," ed. John D. Barry et al., The Lexham Bible Dictionary (Bellingham,

WA: Lexham Press, 2016).

65. M. L. Strauss, "Sadducees," ed. Joel B. Green, Jeannine K. Brown, and Nicholas Perrin, Dictionary of Jesus and the Gospels, Second Edition (Downers Grove, IL; Nottingham, England: IVP Academic; IVP, 2013), 824.

66. Ibid.

67. Anthony J. Saldarini, "Sanhedrin," ed. David Noel Freedman, The Anchor Yale Bible Dictionary (New York: Doubleday, 1992), 975.

68. Anthony J. Saldarini, "Sanhedrin," ed. David Noel Freedman, The Anchor Yale Bible Dictionary (New York: Doubleday, 1992), 976–977.

69. Frank Stagg, "Rendering to Caesar What Belongs to Caesar: Christian Engagement with the World," J Ch St 18 (Winter 1978): 97–102.

70. John S. Feinberg and Paul D. Feinberg, Ethics for a Brave New World (Wheaton, IL: Crossway Books, 1993), 393–394.

71. https://news.gallup.com/poll/350486/record-high-support-same-sex-marriage.aspx

ABOUT REALFAITH

Faith that does not result in good deeds is not real faith. -James 2:20, TLB

With Pastor Mark, it's all about Jesus! He is a spiritual leader, prolific author, and compelling speaker, but at his core, he's a family man. Mark and his wife, Grace, have been married and doing vocational ministry together since 1993 and, along with their five kids, planted Trinity Church in Scottsdale, Arizona as a family ministry.

Pastor Mark, Grace, and their oldest daughter, Ashley, also started RealFaith Ministries, which contains a mountain of Bible teaching for men, women, couples, parents, pastors, leaders, Spanish speakers, and more! You can access it all by visiting **RealFaith. com** or downloading the **RealFaith app**.

With three kids now married and a continued parade of cute grandkids arriving, it's one of his greatest honors to see his adult kids and their families following Jesus, leading their families, and raising their kids to know and love Jesus.

With a master's degree in exegetical theology from Western Seminary in Portland, Oregon, he has spent the better part of his life teaching verse-by-verse through books of the Bible, contextualizing its timeless truths, and never shying away from challenging, convicting passages that speak to the heart of current cultural dilemmas.

Together, Mark and Grace have co-authored *Win Your War, Real Marriage,* and *Real Romance: Sex in the Song of Songs,* and he co-authored a father-daughter project with his daughter, Ashley. Pastor Mark has also written numerous other books including *Spirit-Filled Jesus, Who Do You Think You Are?, Vintage Jesus,* and *Doctrine.* If you have any prayer requests for us, questions for future Ask Pastor Mark or Dear Grace videos, or a testimony regarding how God has used this and other resources to help you learn God's Word, we would love to hear from you at **hello@realfaith.com**.

For more content
from Pastor Mark on
elections, voting, and
other topics in this
book, scan the QR
code below.

IT'S ALL ABOUT JESUS!

realfaith.com

Made in the USA
Coppell, TX
25 September 2024

37716756R00108